COPTIC EGYPT

COPTIC EGYPT
History and Guide
Revised Edition

Jill Kamil

Plans and Maps by Hassan Ibrahim

The American University in Cairo Press

The American University in Cairo Press

Dedicated with love to

Timmy and Tawfik

Ricky and Christine

Dar el Kutub No. 4791/90
ISBN 977 424 242 4

Printed in Egypt by International Press

CONTENTS

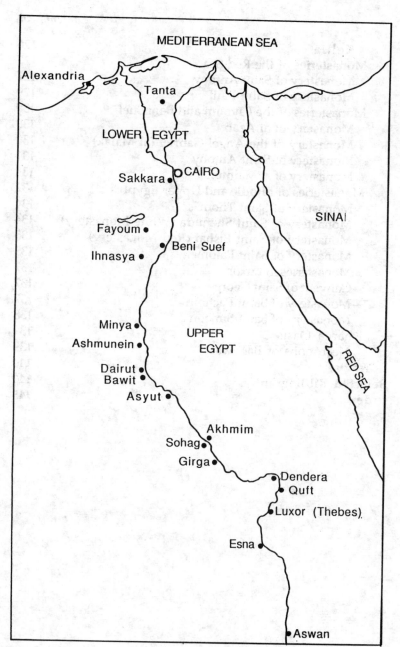

Egypt

ILLUSTRATIONS

PLANS AND MAPS

ACKNOWLEDGMENTS

Many persons, scholars and laymen, have been helpful in contributing ideas in order to bring out this second, revised and enlarged, edition of *Coptic Egypt*, particularly Anba Bishoy, Bishop of Damietta. To all, my grateful thanks, along with the many people who contributed to the first edition, including Professors: Michael Dols, for his suggestions and references concerning the role of the holy man in late antiquity, Ronald Leprohon for reading and commenting on the section on the pharaonic period, and John Rodenbeck for help with the Ptolemaic period. Special thanks are extended also to Barbara Ibronyi for constructive criticism of the chapter on Coptic art, as well as for editing the original manuscript, and to Dr. Gawdat Gabra, director of the Coptic Museum in Cairo, for help and encouragement, and for permission to take photographs in the Coptic Museum.

Limestone stela in the form of a 'naos' showing a seated child holding a bunch of grapes and a bird. Provenance unknown; now in Coptic Museum. Photograph courtesy of Coptic Museum.

FOREWORD

It is a pleasure for me to write a foreword to *Coptic Egypt*, which is the first book that provides the reader with a definitive guide to the most frequently visited Coptic monuments throughout Egypt, and includes a separate chapter on the Coptic Museum, which, with its 14,000 objects, represents the largest collection of Coptic art in the world.

Coptology has become an independent discipline only in the last decades. Hitherto, Coptic studies were included, in different universities, in their departments of Greco–Roman, Near Eastern, or Byzantine studies. Only in 1971 was a professor of Coptology appointed in Münster University in West Germany; and at other universities, especially in Rome, Geneva, and Paris, Coptic studies were limited to the teaching of language and literature.

The general public became more aware of Egypt's Christian heritage when, in 1941, the first exhibition of Coptic art was opened in the United States in the Brooklyn Museum. In 1963 another was opened in West Germany, in Villa Hügel, Essen. These exhibitions familiarized scholars as well as the general public with Coptic art forms, and aroused their interest to know more about this Christian institution. This book will undoubtedly facilitate their understanding and encourage them to visit the sites.

Dr. Gawdat Gabra
Director, Coptic Museum   May 1986

Coptic cross in ivory inlay on wood paneling. Right altar, church of Saint Sergius, Old Cairo. Photograph by Cassandra Vivian.

PREFACE

The word *Copt* derives from the Greek *Aigyptios* ('Egyptian'), via Coptic *Kyptaios* and Arabic *Qibti*. *Aigyptios*, in turn, derives from *Hikaptah* ('House of the *ka* (spirit) of Ptah'), one of the names for Memphis, the first capital of ancient Egypt. The Arab invaders in A.D. 640 called Egypt *dar al Qibt* ('home of the Egyptians') and since Christianity was then the official religion of Egypt, the word *Qibt* came to refer to the practitioners of Christianity as well as to the inhabitants of the Nile Valley.

There has been no Coptic government; the title of this book refers to a culture, a church, and a people. In modern usage the term *Coptic* refers to Orthodox Egyptian Christianity, as well as to the last stage of the ancient Egyptian language, as represented in the script and liturgy of the Coptic church, and to the distinctive art and architecture that developed as an early expression of the new faith.

The Coptic church is one of the oldest in Christendom. According to hallowed tradition, Saint Mark the Evangelist— author of the oldest of the four canonical gospels—preached in Egypt in the first century A.D. and founded churches in Alexandria. Coptic tradition also holds that Saint Mark heads the list of patriarchs of Alexandria, and today's spiritual leader of the Coptic community, Pope Shenuda III, is his 117th successor.

Copts regard theirs as the orthodox church that held firm to the Nicene Creed as formulated in the first and greatest of the church councils. They take pride in the fact that Antony, an Egyptian hermit, remains the spiritual father of Christian

xv

monasticism, and that Athanasius, his disciple, was its first spokesman in the West. All Christian monasticism stems, either directly or indirectly, from the Egyptian example: Saint Basil, organizer of the monastic movement in Asia Minor, and whose rule is followed by the eastern churches, visited Egypt around 357; Saint Jerome, who translated the Bible into Latin, came to Egypt around 400 and left details of his experiences in his letters; Saint Benedict founded monasteries in the sixth century on the model of Saint Pachom (see p.26), but in a stricter form. And countless pilgrims visited the Desert Fathers and emulated their spiritual, disciplined lives. The Ethiopian church is an offshoot of the Coptic church, its bishop having been consecrated by Athanasius in the fourth century. And there is even indication, though no conclusive evidence, of a Coptic missionary movement as far afield as Ireland, since Irish monasticism is closer to that of Saint Pachom than of Saint Benedict.

Although integrated into the body politic of the Egyptian nation, the Copts have survived as a strong religious entity, forming between five and ten percent of the population. They pride themselves on the apostolicity of their church, whose founder, according to Alexandrian tradition, was the first in an unbroken chain of patriarchs.

INTRODUCTION

HISTORICAL BACKGROUND

Egypt for the first two centuries of the Christian era is an extremely complex, heavily documented, yet poorly understood period of history. The reasons for this are manifold but the most important is that the earliest European accounts of this period of Egyptian history, dating from the Middle Ages and the Renaissance, were written from the angle of the occupying power—i.e. Rome and Byzantium. In other words, Christianity was set in a Greek–Roman, not an Egyptian, context. Modern classicists share this prejudice for a number of reasons, one of which is that classical antiquity still provides most of their source material. In other words, Egypt in the early Christian era is presented as a Roman colony, not as a nation with an identity and a tradition that survived Roman occupation. As a result, a sense of continuity has been lost and it is not easy to provide a satisfactory answer to a basic question: how did the Egyptians, with a distinctive civilization, come to accept the divinity of the historical Jesus? Why was Christianity so successful in Egypt?

In order to answer this question, one must go back a thousand years before the Christian era, to the beginning of what is known as the period of decline. Only by tracing this eventful stretch of history, which comprised several distinct phases, can one appreciate the reaction of the people to the unified approach to religion that Christianity offered.

Period of Decline (1080 – 720 B.C.)

Ramses III (1182–1151 B.C.) was the last of the great pharaohs. He conquered the Libyans and repelled invaders

1

from the north, the People of the Sea, but he and his ever-weakening successors fell more and more under the yoke of the priests of Amon. These had grown increasingly wealthy and wielded great power. There were labor problems and strikes, and finally the high priests seized the throne of Egypt in 1080 B.C. Theoretically, the country was still united. In fact the government became synonymous with corruption, and a state of semi-anarchy blighted the land. Occupation by successive foreign military powers was the result, and it is interesting to observe that around this time there is evidence of a subtle change in the religious sentiments of people of the Nile Valley. Personal piety made its appearance. When one thinks of ancient Egypt, its great temples and elaborate ritual, religion at a personal level is difficult to conceive. There is, however, evidence for the relationship between the two. Texts leave no doubt that ordinary people went to national temples to bring their private problems before their local god. In fact, certain important officials, sages, and priests, who raised statues of themselves in temple precincts, were regarded as intermediaries in approaching the deity. "Say a prayer on my behalf" or "invoke my name" are frequent phrases left beside such statues (on ostraca, scraps of papyrus, pieces of wood, sometimes small stelae) by people who journeyed to the temple for the express purpose of submitting personal entreaties.

It is important to note, in view of Christianity's stress on humility, that there is evidence of personal piety at all levels of society. At one end of the scale we find, in the workers' community at Deir al Madina on the Theban necropolis (occupied between about 1184 and 1080 B.C.) funerary monuments bearing such phrases as "poor in spirit," "look upon me and be merciful," and "punish me not for my many sins." At the other extreme, the piety of the pharaoh is depicted in relief (for example in the temple of Seti I at Abydos) in numerous representations where he bends slightly at the waist in reverence before an honored deity. This is a far cry from the all-powerful pharaoh who, for thousands of years, was himself a god.

In 950 B.C., Sheshonk I, from a family of Libyan descent but completely Egyptianized, took power. These Libyans were probably descendants of mercenary troops who had earlier been granted land in return for military service. The Libyan monarchs, who conducted themselves as pharaohs and honored the traditions of Egypt, ruled for two centuries, during which time there appears to have been little further change in the climate of leadership, or in the religious sentiments of the people.

The Beginning of Foreign Occupation

In 720 B.C., Piankhi, a military leader from the region of the fourth cataract (Kush, lower Sudan) marched northward. Since his people had absorbed Egyptian culture during a long period of colonial rule Piankhi did not view himself as a conqueror. In fact, he felt obliged to free Egypt from the forces of barbarism that had engulfed it. The Egyptians, however, did not regard the Kushites as liberators. It was only after a military clash at Memphis, when the Kushites surged over the ramparts of the ancient city, that the Egyptians surrendered. Like the Libyans before them, the Kushites established themselves as genuine pharaohs, restored ancient temples, and were sympathetic to local customs and institutions. There was apparently no difficulty in a foreigner becoming pharaoh. So long as a leader behaved in accordance with tradition, he was accepted.

Monarchical rule was highly personalized. The king was divine, spokesman of the gods, and the personification of *maat*—an abstract term based on the concept of cosmic order and referring to order, truth, and justice. A strong leader had power, being responsible for the country's economy; he had military strength to repel Egypt's enemies; and in hearing appeals and granting petitions he was the supreme judge who exercised *maat*.

In 671 B.C., the Assyrians, who bear the reputation of being the most militaristic and ruthless of ancient peoples, conquered Egypt, putting an end to Kushite rule. With a well-trained army they moved south, from province to province, assuring the local population of a speedy liberation from oppression. But the Egyptians rebelled against the new invaders and drove them north again. The Assyrians staged a counter-attack. They scaled the walls of Memphis and took it by force. Realizing that occupation of Upper Egypt was necessary for the complete pacification of the country, they marched southward again, this time desecrating monuments, killing people, and looting temples. The ancient gods seemed powerless to protect their houses. With shrines destroyed, faith in the priesthood diminished. Moreover, there was already a growing sense that kingship was no longer synonymous with law and order. The peoples' inherent trust and confidence in the pharaoh began to falter. Traditional values were displaced.

After these long centuries of foreign rule, Egypt knew but one short respite: a brilliant revival, known as the Saite Period (664–525 B.C.), when an Egyptian named Psamtik, from the Delta city of Sais, turned his attention to reestablishing a sense of national unity and restating religious ideals and traditions. The unflagging efforts of this great leader and the Saite rulers that followed him to restore order and former greatness led them to pattern their government, religion, and society on the Old Kingdom, a civilization that was already two thousand years old. Little wonder that they failed to satisfactorily reconcile the confident values of the past with the passive values then existing. An increased reverence for sacred animals and birds had developed when the people lost faith in the priesthoods, and the Saite rulers, in their desire to cater to the needs of the population, began to raise sanctuaries to crocodiles, ibises, cats, and bulls. Temples were also built at Memphis, Philae, and Behbet al Hagar in the Delta in honor of the goddess Isis, who was associated with kingship.

Greek immigrants settled in the western Delta, in Sais, and in Memphis during this period, and there was a widespread tendency to cultural integration, including intermarriage between Egyptians and foreigners. Moreover, as communications between Egypt and the Greek states became more frequent, the reputation of Egypt as a land of wonders spread around the Mediterranean world. Greek traders and army recruits alike carried back to their lands tales of the marvelous monuments of Thebes, as well as their respect for the Egyptians' veneration of their ancestors.

Saite rule ended when the Persian king Cambyses occupied Egypt in 525 B.C. and turned Egypt into a Persian province. The new rulers, like the Libyans and the Kushites, at first showed respect for the religion and customs of the country in an effort to gain support. Although there was no great change in the government structure, the Egyptians nevertheless took the earliest opportunity to rout their invaders. Unfortunately, they were able to maintain independence for only about sixty years before the Persian army reconquered Egypt. This time there was less tolerance of local customs—we know for instance that they plundered temples and killed a sacred bull at Memphis. Autobiographical inscriptions of the Persian period reveal an attitude and a piety that, although traditional in many respects, subtly differ from those of the past. The people of Egypt had become more resigned and introspective. There was, for one thing, more concern for the afterlife, over which man had no control.

There were still great centers of learning, especially at Heliopolis and Sais. Among the Greek scholars who are said to have come to Egypt in classical times, and who acknowledged that they learned a great deal from the Egyptian sages, were the statesman and scientist Thales of Miletus, the philosopher and mathematician Pythagoras, the lawyer and poet Solon, and Hecataeus of Miletus, who wrote the first systematic description of the world. Better attested is the visit of Herodotus, the traveler–historian, who devoted the second of his nine history books to research and enquiry into Egypt, gathering information (albeit sometimes from unreliable sources) about the land and the people. Thus before the conquest of Egypt by Alexander the Great, we have evidence of a diverse and cosmopolitan society that ranged from men of learning to the largely illiterate masses, whether Egyptians, Greeks, Macedonians, Persians, Carians, or Jews.

There is also evidence of the growth of personal piety among the ordinary people, as revealed in prayers from the "poor in spirit;" a belief that certain people could act as intermediaries with the divine; a preoccupation with death; and the resuscitation of a mother–goddess cult. This complex society was now to be overlaid with a new Macedonian elite.

Ptolemaic Rule (332–30 B.C.)

When Alexander the Great came to Egypt in 332 B.C. he and his army were welcomed by the Egyptians. He consulted the oracle of Amon at Siwa oasis, which authenticated his divinity and recognized him as the legitimate successor to the ancient pharaohs. Before he left Egypt and met his untimely death at Babylon, Alexander laid out his great city and seaport, Alexandria, so situated as to facilitate the flow of Egypt's surplus resources to the Archipelago and to intercept all trade with Africa and Asia. The city occupied a limestone ridge between Lake Mareotis and the sea, on a site chosen to avoid the problem of silting up by Nile deposits, which are swept to the east by currents. The island of Pharos, with its famous lighthouse, was artificially connected by a causeway to the mainland, and a spacious harbor was formed on the east with enormous potential for maritime trade.

Egypt was held by General Ptolemy when Alexander died in 323 B.C. He took over leadership, first as satrap (a Persian title), then as governor, and finally, in 305 B.C., as King Ptolemy I. During the three centuries of Ptolemaic rule that followed, Egypt was again, for the first time in a thousand years, the seat of a brilliant kingdom. Alexandria, the capital, became the greatest seat of learning in the Mediterranean world. The city was, in fact, to dominate the eastern Mediterranean world politically, culturally, and economically for over six centuries.

A large segment of the population of Alexandria was Jewish. Sizable communities of Jews had been established in Egypt since their expulsion from Jerusalem by Nebuchadnezzar in 586 B.C. They extended, by the time of the Ptolemies, as far south as the island of Elephantine opposite Aswan. When Palestine fell under the control of Ptolemy I in 301 B.C., he brought back Jewish mercenaries who joined the already established communities. Foreigners were welcome, indeed they were encouraged to come and live in Egypt. The immigrants took up residence in Alexandria, the Delta, in certain quarters of Memphis, and in Upper Egypt.

Ptolemy did not continue Alexander's practice of founding cities in deserted or unpopulated areas. In fact, with the exception of Ptolemais (which was named after himself) on the western bank of the Nile in Middle Egypt and the old Greek colony of Naucratis in the Delta, only Alexandria represented a traditional Greek city state. Ptolemy chose instead to settle his mercenary troops (Greeks, Macedonians, Persians, and Hellenized Western Asiatics) among the Egyptian population in or near the capitals of the provinces, as well as in the Fayoum, a fertile depression in the western desert. The result was a cultural amalgam that profoundly affected Egypt. Although a common culture was slowly to emerge, there is evidence, too, of cultural discrimination against Egyptians and an increased sense of national identity among them.

Some Hellenized Egyptians were, in time, to become wealthy members of the community. But there were also men of piety who renounced worldly ideals and practiced asceticism. Above all, the Egyptian priesthood retained its distinctive character. Priests abstained from certain prohibited foods, carried out rituals of purification, and (since the concept of kingship could accommodate the new rulers without difficulty) played an important role in the emergence of a Greek–Egyptian culture. They accepted the identification of Greek gods with Egyptian, performed symbolic acts of homage to the Ptolemaic kings, and ensured that the kings properly performed the necessary rituals at traditional festivals or in laying the foundations of new temples.

The languages in official use in Egypt were Greek and Egyptian, Greek being the more widely used. Egyptian literates had learned Greek long before the conquest by Alexander. They also realized that if they transcribed their own language in the Greek alphabet, which was well known among the middle classes and was simpler to read than demotic (the cursive form of hieroglyphic writing in its latest development), communication would be easier. Scribes started transliterating Egyptian sounds in Greek, adding seven extra letters from the demotic alphabet to accommodate the sounds for which there were no Greek letters. The emergence of this new script, now known as Coptic, cannot be dated precisely. The earliest attempt to write the Egyptian language alphabetically in Greek, feeble but important, has survived in an inscription dating to the Kushite dynasty (750–656 B.C.) at

Abydos. It is important to stress the fact that many Egyptians were bilingual, because surviving textual evidence of Ptolemaic Egypt is largely in Greek and, as a result, one tends to lose sight of the Egyptian identity. About 280 B.C., for example, Ptolemy II commissioned Egyptians to translate their literature into Greek, and Manetho, a Hellenized Egyptian priest who bore a Greek name, wrote the history of his country. He divided it into thirty dynasties from Menes, the legendary founder of the first dynasty, to Alexander the Great, grouping it into three main periods; these dynasties and periods are still the basis of the chronological table we use today. Manetho, and others like him, may have been of minor interest to the Ptolemies, but they illustrate that among the Egyptians there were learned literates with a knowledge of history.

Greek became the mother-tongue of the Jews in Egypt. Unable to speak Hebrew, which had disappeared as a living language, Egyptian Jews may have felt a need to translate their sacred books into Greek. In any case, a translation was supposedly commissioned by Ptolemy II, and, according to the legend, seventy-two translators, chosen from among the most learned Jewish scholars, worked for seventy-two days. This legend explains the traditional name of the Ptolemaic version of the Old Testament, the Septuagint ('seventy'), which is the basis of biblical translations into every European language.

Although, therefore, Egypt was ruled by a Greek-speaking elite, and the bulk of the population was largely illiterate, there was a bilingual community that was multinational. This is nowhere more clearly demonstrated than in a collection of syncretistic treatises known as the *Corpus Hermeticum* (Hermetic literature). The corpus was purportedly written by Thoth, the ancient Egyptian god of wisdom who, under his Greek name Hermes Trismegistus, gave the compilation its name. The Hermetic texts, some composed in Greek, some translated from Egyptian into Greek, were a blend of semi-philosophical treatises on the divine, ancient Egyptian wisdoms and literature, and esoteric teachings including cosmological conceptions and mysticism. Through such literature, one can best appreciate the varied and subtle ways in which consciousness of the divine manifested itself among the whole cultural amalgam in Egypt.

The Ptolemies regarded Egypt as their land and they played a dual role in it, conducting themselves as both Greeks and 'legitimate' kings of Egypt. The roles were separate, yet interrelated. As Greeks they resided in Alexandria, the great intellectual center where research, especially with practical aims, was fostered. Ptolemy III issued an important decree that all travelers disembarking at Alexandria should have taken from them and placed in the Library any literature in their baggage, in exchange for an official certified copy. Since distinguished astronomers, mathematicians, geographers, historians, poets, and philosophers gravitated to the Museum attached to the Library, it became a vitally important research institution.

Yet the Ptolemies as pharaohs meanwhile lavished revenues on local priesthoods for the upkeep of temples, or at least exempted them from taxes. They were quick to realize the benefits of leaving to trained Egyptians the tasks that they had carried on for thousands of years, especially in the assessment and collection of taxes, and they accepted the Egyptian administrative divisions of the country into provinces (*nomes* in Greek), each under a governor (*nomarch*). Although the nome capitals were towns of some considerable size, they had no self-government and were probably regarded by the Greeks as not much more than villages, despite the designation *polis*: Hermopolis, 'the city of Hermes' (modern Ashmunein), for example, and Hierakleopolis, 'the city of Heracles' (modern Ihnasya, to the south of the Fayoum).

Egyptian society had always been highly stratified. It ranged from the noble class, through the priestly scribes and learned literates, down the bureaucratic scale to the farming masses. Superimposed on Egyptian society were the ruling Greeks and their officials who resided in Alexandria and the Greek city-states, as well as the thousands of settled Greek and Macedonian soldiers, merchants, businessmen, traders, artisans, and manual laborers, many of whom married Egyptians and whose children, by the second and third generations, bore both Greek and Egyptian names. To this diversified population one must not forget to add the Persian and Jewish settlers.

To provide a link between his Greek and Egyptian subjects, Ptolemy I had introduced a new cult, that of Serapis, a hybrid deity. He observed that the Apis bull was worshiped at Memphis, which was even then a thriving religious center, and he assumed, wrongly, that the cult was popular and widespread. The deceased Apis was known as Osiris–Apis, or Oserapis, from which Serapis was derived. It is presumed that Ptolemy supplied Serapis with anthropomorphic features and declared him to be the national god. To launch the new deity on his career, he declared that he had had a dream in which a colossal statue was revealed to him. No sooner did he communicate his revelation to the people than a statue of Serapis was put on view, closely resembling his vision: a man with curly hair, a long beard, and a benign expression. The cult of Serapis was to have sweeping success throughout Greece and Asia Minor, in Sicily, and especially in Rome. In Egypt, Serapis was most widely worshiped in Alexandria and Memphis, where the temple of Serapis, the Serapeum, on the Sakkara necropolis became one of the most famous sites in Egypt.

Egypt's other deities were identified with those of Greece. The god at Thebes, Amon–Ra, was identified with Zeus, supreme god of Olympus, and Amon's wife, Mut, with Hera, Zeus' consort and queen of the sky. The Egyptian Horus was easily identified with Apollo, both being sun-gods. Thoth, the Egyptian god of wisdom said to have invented writing, was associated with Hermes, messenger of Zeus. Osiris, god of the underworld, became one with Hades of the Greek underworld, while Isis, beloved wife of Osiris and mother of Horus, was identified with the earth-mother Demeter. This pantheon of gods enabled the Egyptians and Egyptianized Greeks to worship the same gods in the same temples, under different names. It should be added, however, that Greeks also accepted the efficacy of Egypt's local deities under their traditional names, and openly went to sacred temples to receive oracles. When Ptolemy II started reconstruction of the temple of Isis begun by the Saite kings on the island of Philae south of Aswan, it became a popular healing center. In fact the cult of this goddess later swept the Mediterranean world.

Out of the interaction between Greeks and Egyptians at many levels, both intellectual and popular, a Greek–Egyptian culture emerged. It is important to note the Egyptian element in this common culture because it provides the link, the historical continuity we shall trace in the growth of the Coptic church. In other words, although Greeks ruled Egypt, and a number of Egyptians absorbed Greek culture and became Hellenized, making their contributions to the Mediterranean world, yet Greeks, while many were Egyptianized, could never be part of Egypt's national heritage. They remained a breed apart.

When the Ptolemies assumed religious office and, like the ancient pharaohs, made ceremonial journeys up the Nile to make offerings at temples; when they were depicted in these temples (which were built on traditional lines) in the manner of the ancient pharaohs, duly equipped with names and titles in hieroglyphics; and when they showed their readiness to accept symbolic acts of homage by the Egyptians because they realized that leadership was a feature of the central religious organization that had long existed in Egypt; it is interesting to observe that through these acts they not only continued ancient traditions, but, in helping maintain the Egyptian sense of prestige, helped also to preserve the class of priests and scribes who carried forward Egyptian thought and ancient ritual.

Therefore, despite the welding of Greek and Egyptian cultures, and evidence of some Egyptians being drawn upwards into the new dominant elite, there is surprisingly little evidence of the penetration of Greek elements into traditional Egyptian society. True, the Greeks had identified their gods with Egyptian gods and worshiped them in the same temples, but there were few Greek-named priests in the local cults. These were invariably Egyptians. The scales tilted, therefore, towards the dominance of Greek culture, with the inevitable subordination of the Egyptian. In other words, the Ptolemies turned the Egyptians into second-class citizens. There developed, consequently, a strong anti-Egyptian feeling among the educated Greeks. Although they held the Egyptian culture in reverence in many ways, they did not bother to learn the Egyptian language or writing, and they did not encourage Egyptians to become citizens of Alexandria and the Greek cities.   Papyri found in the cities provide a wealth of documentary evidence that clearly reflects Greek disdain for the Egyptians.

Neither should anti-Greek feeling among the Egyptians, however, be underestimated. The Egyptians had a strong sense of cultural superiority to anyone who did not speak their language, as Herodotus remarked even in Persian times. To be sure, some Egyptian priests and officials collaborated with the Ptolemies, as evidenced by such documents as the Canopic Decree, but there is also indication that Egyptians resented being treated as a conquered race, and rebelled frequently. One Upper Egyptian province in particular, the Thebaid (Luxor), remained most ardently nationalistic as the Ptolemies' unequal treatment of their subjects led to ever more frequent Egyptian revolts. Egyptians brought suits against Greeks, and Greeks against Egyptians. Prophetic writings were widely circulated promising Egyptians expulsion of the foreigners.

Although, therefore, a Greek–Egyptian culture had emerged out of generations of contact, differences remained, and hostility grew. The progressively diminishing respect of the Egyptians for the ruling power was such that a man called Ptolemy, who lived in the reign of Ptolemy IV (222–205 B.C.) and whose papers were found in the ruins of the Serapeum in Alexandria, complained bitterly of attacks made on him "because I am a Greek." Amusing evidence of the Egyptian sense of superiority appears in a text in which Egyptians are instructed, after having cursed the head of a sacrificial lamb, to either cast it into the Nile or sell it to the Greeks!

Egyptians who were not Hellenized acquired, by the last century of Ptolemaic rule, a position that was somewhat nearer equality with the Greeks than they had enjoyed under the earlier Ptolemies. Egyptian veterans received allotments of land like the Greeks, which may have come about due to rival claimants to the throne rallying the Egyptians for popular support. Whatever the reason, it is important to note the appearance of a landed, wealthy Egyptian segment of the population, because it was among them that the most ardent nationalism was born. Indeed, it was they who were to suffer most severely under the Romans, and it was from their ranks that some of Coptic Christianity's greatest spiritual leaders emerged.

Towards the end of the second century B.C. there were economic problems and civil unrest in Egypt, along with a decline in foreign commerce resulting from the loss of Egypt's possessions in and around the Aegean and in Syria. The last of the Ptolemies were weak leaders and the prosperity of the kingdom declined. The court, rich in material wealth and lax in morals, became the scene of decadence and anarchy.

Men of piety began to renounce worldly concerns and devote themselves to lives of spiritual contemplation and prayer. This phenomenon occurred centuries before the Christian era in Egypt and Palestine, as well as in Persia and India, where the practices of ascetics had been observed by Alexander. In Egypt, such devotees lived in places of strict seclusion in the desert and in ancient tombs, while in Palestine evidence of their way of life has been found in caves near the Dead Sea. Such hermits became known as *anchorites* (from the Greek root meaning to retire or withdraw). The term originally referred to those who withdrew from labor, but by the first century B.C. it came to describe anti-materialistic ascetics who lived in isolated seclusion. These were the pre-Christian forerunners of great spiritual leaders like Saint Paul, Saint Antony, and Saint Pachom.

Roman Occupation

Towards the end of the Ptolemaic period Egypt was condemned to impotence by the degenerate leaders who luxuriated in their rich and sumptuous courts and were grossly, even violently, intolerant of the local population. The Egyptians staged periodic revolts, but these were apathetic demonstrations and had little effect. Egypt had begun to fall more and more under the influence of Rome, which was by now a vast power with expanding interests across the sea. After Antony's defeat at Actium and Cleopatra's subsequent suicide at Alexandria, Egypt became a province of the Roman Empire.

From the beginning of Roman rule in Egypt there were pitched battles from Alexandria to Thebes. Although the

Roman emperors claimed to be successors of the ancient pharaohs, it is clear that the Egyptians did not regard them as such. Not only did they live in far-off Rome and appoint a prefect, or representative, to the position formerly held in the scheme of government by the king, but the prefect did not perform the ceremonial functions of divine kingship as the Ptolemaic kings had. As a result, there was a drastic change in the climate of leadership. Further, the emperor Augustus aroused the ire of the Greeks in Alexandria when he abolished the Greek senate and took administrative powers away from Greek officials, but granted self-government to the Jews. The Greeks, who had founded the great capital, had distrusted Roman ambition from the beginning. Their formal request to Augustus to retract the privileges granted the Jews was ignored. Fighting soon broke out, first between Greeks and Jews, then with the Romans when they tried to separate the two. The unrest that marks the beginning of the Christian era in Alexandria had already begun. Ships in the harbor were set on fire and the flames spread to the Museum. The destruction of the main Library in the palace, in which an estimated 490,000 rolls of papyrus perished, may have occurred at this time.

The Romans thenceforth stationed garrisons at Alexandria, which remained the capital; at Babylon (Old Cairo), which was the key to communications with western Asia and Lower Egypt; and at Syene (Aswan), which was Egypt's southern boundary. They controlled Egypt by force, and regarded the land as no more than a granary supplying wheat to Rome. Consequently, an enormous burden of taxation was placed on the people of the Nile Valley. A census was imposed on villages throughout the land and house-to-house registration of the number of residents was made. This might have been considered normal procedure in Rome, but it was regarded by Egyptians as an infringement of their privacy. Calculations of the wheat quota were based, not on the productivity of the land, but on the number of men in a village.

Egyptians who had enjoyed certain privileges under the later Ptolemies, and acquired considerable wealth, received no special consideration from the Romans. Indeed, their problems were compounded when the emperor Trajan declared that peasant farmers should be recruited for the Roman army. Although Hadrian reduced rentals on imperial lands, and exempted Greek settlers in the Fayoum and citizens of Greek cities from taxation, the people of rural Egypt were discriminated against. Their taxes were assessed at a flat rate, without regard to income, age, or capacity for work. When men fled or hid, the Romans discovered a cruel way to coerce their families into revealing their whereabouts— aware of the value set by the Egyptians on proper mummification and internment of their dead, they seized bodies and held them ransom. Such evidence dates from the reigns of the emperors Caligula and Claudius in the first half of the first century A.D. As early as the time of the emperor Nero (A.D. 54–68) there are records of men having "fled leaving no property"—forty-three in number, then sixty, then a hundred from a single village. As terror and disillusionment spread, hope was abandoned, and more men turned from cruel political reality to a life of contemplation and prayer.

The Romans made an overt show of respect for Egyptian priesthoods by constructing new or completing older temples begun by the Ptolemies. The temple to the goddess Hathor at Dendera, for example, which was begun before the reign of Ptolemy VIII, was completed some 150 years later under the emperor Tiberius. And temples in the traditional style were completed at Esna, Kom Ombo, and Philae. It is worthy of note, however, that the sites for these temples were chosen for their strategic position as well as for the sake of ancient tradition. Esna had been a center for local commerce from earliest times; Kom Ombo, situated on a bend in the Nile, commanded the trade routes to Nubia in the south; and Philae was situated on Egypt's southern border. Establishing cult centers and a satisfied local population consequently served Roman ends.

Temple lands elsewhere, however, were annexed and placed under the control of the Roman government. Local priests were allotted only a small part of sacred property and their own material wealth was curbed. The produce of vineyards, palm groves, and fig plantations owned by temples was collected by Roman officials, and taxes were levied on sheep, oxen, horses and donkeys. A Roman official now held the title of High

Priest of Alexandria and all Egypt and was the supreme authority over all the temples.

The institution of sacrosanct monarchy, a cardinal feature of Egyptian life in pharaonic times which had been maintained by various later dynasties, was lost in Roman times. The emperors may have claimed to be divine but it was their prefects who ruled Egypt, reduced the prestige of the priests, and exerted pressure on the people. They siphoned off the wealth of the land to Rome and recruited Egyptians to fight Roman wars in other countries. The Egyptians, who had accepted Ptolemaic rule, resisted Roman. It is not difficult to see the difference between them. Under the Ptolemies, Egypt had retained its integrity and had had a stable economy. Under the Romans, the country was shorn of identity and impoverished. It was no more than a private estate of the emperor and a pleasure-ground for the Roman upper classes, who visited Egypt in vast numbers. Romans traveled on luxurious Nile cruises to see the Pyramids of Giza, one of the seven wonders of the ancient world, and visit such attractions as the statue, on the Theban necropolis, of Amenhotep III, known to them as the Colossus of Memnon because at dawn each day it gave off strange sounds that they interpreted as Memnon, the legendary son of Aurora, greeting his mother. But they did not settle in Egypt as had the Greeks, and they turned a blind eye to the poverty and want around them. The Egyptians were pressed to maximum production to meet the wheat shipments to Rome, while Roman tourists traveled to healing centers such as Deir al Bahari and the temple of Isis on Philae.

The cult of Egypt's most beloved goddess, Isis, exerted a strong influence on the early Christian church. Along with the cults of Serapis and Osiris it had long ago spread to Rome and had become very popular. As a mother-goddess who protected her son Horus from those who would do him harm and as the devoted wife of Osiris, participating in the mysteries concerning his death and resurrection, Isis was in fact the main competitor with Christianity in Rome until the fourth century. The Roman Republic had tried, unsuccessfully, to suppress the cult and its esoteric mysteries, but the annual festival of Isis (*navigium Isidis*) continued to be celebrated there, even under Christian emperors. In Egypt, the temple of Isis remained a focal point of worship until the reign of Justinian (527–565), when it was closed down.

The stage was set, in the last years of paganism, for the coming of Christianity. Egypt under the Romans had been reduced to the role of a granary. Men of spiritual inclination had withdrawn from the world of materialism to seek perfection in the isolated solitude of the eastern and western deserts. Leadership in its traditional sense had been lost and the prestige of the priests undermined. Moreover, the bulk of the population had little hope of reprieve from their sufferings, because the steady and remorseless eroding of the walls of custom and tradition had left them unsure and unprotected. There was a spiritual void where the past seemed beyond recall and the future without hope. It was this void that Christianity filled. The people readily embraced a doctrine that offered hope, and that preached mercy and brotherhood. According to the Gospel of Saint Matthew, the Holy Family fleeing the wrath of Herod sought refuge in Egypt, and many Copts believe that even before the public ministry of Jesus, Egyptians accepted the Divine Child as lord over their lives.

1

EARLY CHRISTIANITY

According to honored tradition Saint Mark brought Christianity to Egypt in the reign of the Roman emperor Nero in the first century. Some of the earliest converts to the new faith undoubtedly came from the Jewish community in Egypt, which represented the largest concentration of Jews outside Palestine. In fact, tradition also holds that Saint Mark's first convert was a Jewish shoemaker in Alexandria.

Evidence of the diffusion of the new faith in the early centuries is, nevertheless, scanty. This holds true not only in Egypt but all over the Roman world, and may be partly attributable to the need to conceal any connection with the persecuted sect. Another reason is that official documents did not require mention of religious affiliation. The fact that Christianity did spread well beyond Alexandria within half a century of Saint Mark's arrival there is, nevertheless, clear from a fragment of New Testament writings known as the Rylands Papyrus, which was found near Bahnasa in Middle Egypt. It dates no later than the middle of the second century and is part of the Gospel of Saint John, written in Greek. The significance of the discovery is that it provides evidence that Christian literature was being produced and circulated in Middle Egypt at that early date.

Although Egypt before the Christian era was by definition a pagan country, and although the spiritual climate was one of disillusionment, where the people, under the yoke of imperial Rome, craved salvation, there was a stream of traditional thought and belief that prepared the way for the Christian message. An Egyptian text written in demotic and known as the Insinger Papyrus (now in Leiden), dating to the first century, shows that there was not an unbridgeable abyss between pharaonic (pagan) Egypt and the early Christian period in the concept of God. The text is of the genre of ancient Egyptian instruction literature, and is believed to be a collection of popular works transmitted in numerous copies. It shows that the Egyptians, even after the loss of their independence and with their profound sense of malcontentedness, continued to believe in, and to teach, an all-embracing cosmic order which governed human existence. It shows that they had, deeply rooted in their tradition, the belief in a world-creator who was also a creator of order in nature. The twenty-fourth instruction, "the teaching of knowing the greatness of the god, so as to put it in your heart," includes the following verses:

> *When people raise their hands the god knows it.*
> *He knows the impious man who thinks of evil.*
> *He knows the godly man and that he has the greatness of god*
> *in his heart.*
> *He gives good judgement through the counsel which*
> *no one knows.*
> *He creates abundant value without there being a storehouse*
> *behind him.*
> *It is he who makes the way safe without there being a guard.*
> *It is he who gives the just law without there being a judgement.*
> *The hidden work of the god, he makes it known on the earth daily.*
> *He created light and darkness . . .*
> *He created the earth, begetting millions . . .*
> *He created day, month, year . . .*
> *He created summer and winter . . .*
> *He created food before those who are alive, the wonder of the fields.*
> *He created the breath in the egg where there is no access to it.*
> *He created sleep to end weariness.*
> *He created remedies to end illness.*
> *Great is the counsel of the god in putting one thing after another.*
> *The fate and fortune that come, it is the god who sends them.*
> (Papyrus Insinger, *Ancient Egyptian Literature*, Lichtheim, M.,
> Vol III, p.184f.)

Another example of the stream of traditional thought and belief from ancient Egypt through to the Egypt in which Christianity took root is the striking similarity between Akhenaten's hymn to the sun-disc Aten and Psalm 104 of the Old Testament. Akenaten's hymn is especially remarkable when one realizes that it was written long before the Insinger Papyrus, and dates, in fact, to 1,355 years before the Christian era:

> *How manifold is that which thou hast made,*
> *Hidden from view!*
> *Thou sole god, there is no other like thee!*
> *Thou didst create the earth according to thy will, being alone.*
> (Akhenaten's hymn)

> *How manifold are thy works, O Yahweh!*
> *All of them thou hast made by wisdom,*
> *The earth is full of thy creations.*
> (Psalm 104:24)

* * *

> *When thou dost set in the western horizon,*
> *The earth is in darkness, like to death. . . .*
> *Every lion has come forth from his lair;*
> *All the reptiles bite.*
> (Akhenaten's hymn)

> *Thou appointest darkness, that it may be night,*
> *In which all the beasts of the forest prowl:*
> *The young lions roaring for their prey,*
> *To seek their food from God.*
> (Psalm 104:20–21)

The biblical story of Jesus' sojourn in Egypt provides yet another example of continuity. Numerous sites in the Nile Delta and Valley are hallowed as places where the Holy Family hid, rested, or refreshed themselves: there is little doubt that the similarity between the stories of Isis, Egypt's popular mother-goddess protecting her child from his enemies, and of the Virgin Mother escaping with the Child from Herod, was the reason that such a large number of sites came to be sacred. A highly religious society does not suddenly change. The Egyptians readily embraced Christianity because of its affinity with a much older tradition.

The Catechetical School of Alexandria

The first important institution of religious learning in Christian antiquity was the Catechetical School in Alexandria. It was founded by Pantaenus, a Christian scholar who is believed to have come to Alexandria about 180. The scope of the school he founded was not limited to theology: science, mathematics, and the humanities were taught there too. Coptic tradition holds that the distinguished teachers or graduates of the school became patriarchs, and the 'guardians of orthodoxy.'

Clement (160–215), a convert from paganism who succeeded Pantaenus as head of the school, taught in Alexandria for more than twenty years. By the year 190, the church of Alexandria was communicating with the churches of Jerusalem and Antioch concerning such important matters as the date of Easter. There were already some forty bishoprics in Alexandria and Lower Egypt and, as already noted, evidence of the diffusion of the faith in Middle Egypt. Under Clement, and Pantaenus before him, the Psalms and selected writings from the New Testament were translated from Greek into Coptic.

It is interesting to note that although Clement wrote positively about the Hermetic literature, allowing that it constituted a range of material available for the education of priests, he was not so tolerant towards the Gnostics (see below) and their 'heresies.' Although many scholars see Clement as a Gnostic himself, he was, in fact, bitterly critical of the movement.

Clement was succeeded in the Catechetical School around 201 by Origen, a man of pure Coptic stock. Origen was regarded by early church historians as the greatest of the early Christian apologists. He joined the school at an early age, attended lectures by Pantaenus and Clement, and later taught there for twenty-eight years. Like Clement, he was highly critical of the Gnostic movement. Origen traveled far afield, to Rome, Antioch, Athens, and Palestine, where the bishops invited him to deliver public lectures in the churches. He wrote extensively, and his works, along with those of Clement, have occupied a prominent place in the teaching of the universal church for fifteen centuries.

Gnostic Communities

The origin of the Gnostic (from the Greek *gnosis*, knowledge) communities is obscure and until recently not much was known about them. The reason is that when, in the fourth century, the Gnostics were hounded into silence in the name of orthodox Christianity, their writings were destroyed whenever they could be found. Consequently, vital evidence on the early dissemination of the Christian faith among such communities is lacking. Fortunately, a collection of manuscripts bound into codices, or books, was discovered near Nag Hammadi in Upper Egypt in 1945. These texts have raised important issues about the development of Christianity in Egypt. They were copies of original writings that cannot be dated with certainty, though some may go back to as early as the second half of the first century.

The twelve Nag Hammadi codices, or the Nag Hammadi library as they are now known, were collections of writings translated into Coptic. They vary widely in content representing a syncretic spectrum of heritages: local Egyptian concepts and folklore, ancient literature and mystery cults of the Greco–Roman world, Greek philosophy, Persian mysticism, the Old and the New Testaments. The range of literature is astonishing. The codices include: the Gospel of Thomas, which was a secret 'heretical' gospel that did not find its way into the canon of the New Testament; a compilation of sayings attributed to Jesus, with the claim that the words were spoken by the living (post-resurrection) Jesus to Thomas Didymus Judas; extracts from Plato's *Republic*; and apocrypha (literally 'secret books') on Zoroaster and Manichaeism. Little wonder that the Gnostics came under violent attack from both the defenders of Greek philosophy and orthodox Christians.

The Gnostic communities could well be described as a microcosm of the pluralistic society to be seen in areas where

Egypt's diversified population (Egyptians, Jews, Persians, Macedonians, and Greeks) lived and shared beliefs that had merged in a syncretistic alliance. Already the codices have revealed that the movement was not only far more widespread but also of greater historical consequence than was previously thought. They include numerous teachings, treatises, revelations, acts, and gospels, some (like the Gospel of Philip, the Gospel of Truth, and the Gospel of the Egyptians) hitherto unknown. From this material it may be possible to reconstruct a 'Gnostic New Testament,' which some scholars feel may be closer to the original spirit of Jesus. For although it was reasoned by some of the first scholars who worked on the material that since the gospels were heretical, they must have been written later than the gospels of the New Testament, a Harvard scholar, Professor Helmut Koester, has recently suggested otherwise; he maintains that the collection of sayings in the Gospel of Thomas, although compiled around 140, may include some traditions even older than the canonical gospels, "possibly as early as the second half of the first century."

Religious Persecution

The rapid spread of Christianity was undoubtedly accelerated by the conditions prevailing in Egypt under Roman rule. For example, the emperor Septimius Severus, the military commander who was strong enough to hold together the Roman Empire for nearly two decades, decreed in 202 that municipal councils should be set up in all the nome capitals. The purpose, from the point of view of the Romans, may have been to upgrade the status of the Egyptians, but the Egyptians themselves saw the measure as restrictive and resisted it. Consequently, they were severely penalized and faced threats and intimidation from the Romans. A new wave of brutality started, especially in areas where Roman presence was strongest, and many Egyptians sought refuge in the desert, where the spirit of Christianity was growing.

Under the emperor Decius (249–251) Christians were ordered to participate in pagan worship in the presence of Roman officers and to submit certificates of sacrifice. They were required to provide documentary proof that they were not practicing Christians by signing statements to the effect that they and their families made sacrifices to the local gods and had also poured libations in the temple and tasted offerings. Those who refused were declared to be self-avowed Christians and were tortured. Some Christians, in fear for their safety, sent in false certificates, but many were willing to die rather than abjure their faith. Eusebius of Caesarea, in his *History of the Church*, described a rush to martyrdom in Thebes. He wrote that the Christians were "unconcerned in the face of terrors and the varied forms of tortures . . . and receiving sentence of death with joy and laughter and gladness; so that they sang and sent up hymns of thanksgiving to the God of the Universe even to the very last breath." The Coptic *Synaxarium*, containing selected biographies of martyrs and saints for each day of the year, is full of stories of such sufferings. The Decian persecution, which was fortunately cut short by the death of the emperor in battle, was the first systematic attempt to put an end to Christianity by depriving the church of both its leaders and its followers.

It is important to note that the Christian church celebrates both martyrs and confessors, the latter being those who did not suffer the extreme penalty of death. For although hundreds, maybe thousands, died, there was an equal number who escaped, taking their zeal for Christianity with them to create new converts.

Beginning of Monasticism

By the third century thousands of anchorites—ascetics whose original models may be traced to pre-Christian times—were living either alone or in small groups. This *ermitism*, the hermit life, developed simultaneously in Palestine and in the deserts of Egypt. When Paul (228–343) and Antony (251–356), two of Egypt's earliest and best known spiritual leaders, took to a life of meditation and prayer in the mountains along the Red Sea coast, many hermits found in them the spiritual guidance they sought. Paul and Antony, in their separate locations, gave instruction in an atmosphere of security and spirituality. There were no written rules under what has become known as Antonian monasticism. Saint Antony simply gave his disciples two principles that had been revealed to him in a vision: prayer and work. And he introduced monastic garb, a tunic of flax fastened by a leather belt, and an outer sheepskin cloak when needed. The hermits could continue to live in isolated caves, but they came together for spiritual guidance on Saturdays and Sundays.

Ascetic leaders were sometimes of simple origins, like Paul; sometimes they came from among the class of successful landowners, like Antony, whose family had a certain status in the society. It is important to stress that wealthy landowners as well as simple farmers became hermits, because when such people renounced their material possessions they were regarded as having a special power and relationship with the divine. Faith in traditional leadership had long been lost in Egypt, and the early fathers became heroes in whom divine power was believed to be vested. As the reputations of the spiritual leaders grew, the number of their followers increased, and this made it difficult for them to find the seclusion they craved.

Diocletian's Reforms and Persecutions

The reforms of Diocletian mark a turning-point in the history of Christianity. In the year 284, the Roman army elected him emperor, and the appalling social and economic conditions throughout the empire led him to drastically reorganize it along military lines. In Egypt, he divided the land into three major provinces and separated civil and military powers. Then he imposed new methods of tax assessment based on units of productivity. Egyptians were forced into public service and, to facilitate control, Latin was introduced as the official language, even in provinces where Greek had hitherto been used for official documents. Unification of the Roman Empire was undoubtedly the reason for these reforms, but the Egyptians had had enough and rebelled forcefully. The Christians were regarded by the Romans as the subversive element behind the rebellion, and Diocletian decided that if they could not be subjugated, they should be eliminated. They were dismissed from government service, their property was confiscated and their houses were leveled. Search was made for Christian literature, and copies of the Scriptures, when found, were burned. Thousands of people, unable to support these increasingly difficult conditions, fled from their villages. Many joined the existing Christian communities, whose numbers grew.

One of the most widely revered virgin-martyrs of Egypt is Dimiana, a girl of great beauty who became a Christian at the age of fifteen, built a nunnery (with the aid of her father, who was a wealthy governor), and lived in seclusion with forty nuns until all were slaughtered. Apparently the enraged Diocletian, furious at the refusal of Dimiana's father to make a sacrifice to the gods, wreaked vengeance on his child and the nuns, who, despite cruel torture, would not yield and were eventually beheaded. Another renowned martyr from this time was Menas, an army officer born of a good family, who refused to renounce Christianity and was beheaded and buried near Maryut (Mareotis in Greek). There he became a much revered figure, and his church a center of miracles and pilgrimage (see p.120).

Ancient martyrologies may give exaggerated numbers of people who suffered death during the nine years of the Diocletian persecution; nevertheless, in the Theban area it was said to have been so inhuman that at any one time dozens of men were slain along with their wives and children. So harsh is their recollection of the Diocletian era that the Copts later adopted a calendar called the Calendar of the Martyrs, which begins its era on August 29 (or according to the Gregorian calendar September 11), 284, in commemoration of those who died for their faith.

Early Monastic Reform

An important development in the history of the Coptic church, and also a significant factor in the mass conversion of Egypt, was the rise and rapid growth of the monastic movement following the reforms of Diocletian. The semi-cenobitic communities that had grown up around such spiritual leaders as Saint Paul and Saint Antony were replaced by a much stricter form of monasticism.

Saint Pachom (Pachomius in Greek, Anba Bakhum in Arabic), an Upper Egyptian born to pagan parents about 285, was one of Egypt's greatest spiritual leaders and the founder of a form of monasticism that took his name. He was the first to see the benefits of unifying the widely-spread Christian communities.

Pachom was a native Egyptian, who learned Greek only late in life in order to communicate with strangers with whom he came into contact. He seems to have been recruited into the Roman army stationed at Thebes, though he did not remain in it for long, and the reason for his leaving is obscure. According to a fourth-century Coptic chronicler he was released from a Roman prison in 320, became a professed Christian, and was baptized by, and became a disciple of, an aged hermit called Palomen. Palomen, a great spiritual leader in Upper Egypt, was one of the earliest anchorites in the region of Nag Hammadi. He was said to have died from excessive fasting. After Pachom had undergone a period of religious training, and as a result of a vision, he and a group of followers left Palomen's community to establish one of their own, near Akhmim.

The caves in the hills flanking the Nile floodplain in Middle Egypt were populated with large numbers of hermits. Pachom slowly drew them together in a walled complex and began to formulate a rule to govern their daily lives. The monastery was a strict cenobitic (from the Greek for 'common' and 'life') community, a far cry from the anchorites who lived in isolated seclusion, and different from the ever-expanding loosely-knit Antonian communities.

Pachom's monastery was planned from the start with communal facilities such as kitchens, bakeries, water-cisterns, wine presses, and workshops. Pachom introduced a schedule of activities for every hour of the day and night: the time to sleep, rise, pray, eat, and work. He emphasized that a healthy body provided a healthy spirit and he saw to it that there should be no excesses of any kind, not even of spiritual meditation. His aim was to establish a pious, enlightened, and self-sufficient community that would set an example to others.

An applicant for admission to Pachom's monastery did not have to exhibit spectacular feats of mortification of the flesh. Although there are numerous examples of physical self-torture in the lives of the Desert Fathers, a candidate for Pachomian monasticism merely had to undergo a period of probation, after which he was clothed in the habit of a monk and officially joined the community. The monks were grouped into 'houses' or 'settlements' within the monastery, each according to trade or activity. A supervisor was responsible for each house. No visitors were allowed. When Pachom's own sister Mary came to see her brother, she was refused entry to the monastery. Pachom sent a message with the gatekeeper: "You have heard that I am living, therefore grieve not that you did not see me. But, if you would renounce the world and find mercy with God, you shall possess your soul. And I trust the Lord to call unto you many who would join you . . . ." Mary, inspired by her brother's words, chose a cave near his monastery, and women of similar inclination came to her. Pachom appointed a teacher called Peter for the women, an aged monk noted for his piety and devotion. They were instructed in exactly the same rules as those laid down for the men.

The ordered, disciplined cenobitic community under Pachom's spiritual guidance was so successful that he established a second, similar institution. It is not without interest that he chose to found this at Faw Qibli (Pbow), not far west of Gebel al Tarif at Nag Hammadi, where a large Gnostic community flourished. Perhaps Pachom thought to attract some of the more conservative members to his monastery. Be that as it may, Pachom then moved on and established another community, and yet another, until there were no less than eleven Pachomian monasteries in Upper Egypt, including two convents for women. Pachomian monasticism was made known to the West through the writings of Saint Jerome. He was inspired by the fact that the monks were not endeavoring, through solitary and contemplative devotion, merely to save their own souls. He observed that they encouraged the rural population to come to them for spiritual guidance or healing.

Records show that after the death of Pachom there was a short disruption in the monastic movement. Shortly thereafter, however, when monasteries and convents were built in great number, new communities began to follow the rule of Pachom's ideal community instead of a semi-cenobitic organization.

Saint Shenuda (333–451) was another great Coptic reformer, who became one of the most important monks of his day. He worked for eighty years in the White and Red Monasteries in Middle Egypt (see p.134–135), cenobitic communities originally founded by his uncle Pjol with a reputed 2,200 monks and 1,800 nuns under his spiritual guidance. The monasteries of Pjol were run along similar lines to those of Pachom. When Shenuda succeeded his uncle, he reorganized and enlarged the monasteries, and proved to be not only a great spiritual leader but also a positive social reformer. He rendered important services to the community, including opening the doors of the White Monastery during times of famine, providing medical treatment (especially for eye ailments), solving social problems, and providing a weekly meal for anyone who needed it. He also made the first determined effort to stamp out the last remnants of pagan worship from Egypt, especially the worship of relics. Shenuda, who was a prolific writer, was a strong influence on the community in Middle Egypt. His religious guidance and charitable institution were so inspiring that even after his death thousands of people continued to come to the monastery.

Meanwhile, in Lower Egypt, another type of monasticism developed under Saint Amon and Saint Macarius the Great in Wadi al Natrun (see p.122). There, several disciples lived together in isolated *cellia*, or cells, in remote areas in the desert, but not too far from Alexandria. Wadi al Natrun is associated with the great church fathers Moses the Black, Pambo, and the two Macarii; and many of the earliest church fathers, including Saint Gregory the Theologian (329–389), Saint Basil the Great (330–379), Saint Chrysostom (347–407), and Saint Jerome (342–420) visited the area. The *Apophthegmata Patrum*, or Sayings of the Fathers, come from Wadi al Natrun.

Conversion and Controversy

The famous revelation of the emperor Constantine in 312, which resulted in his conversion to Christianity, was followed in 313 by the Edict of Milan, which established the principle of religious toleration, and Christianity was officially recognized in Egypt and throughout the Roman

Empire. It was at last safe to admit to being a Christian, and out of the catacombs and caves came many monks and hermits to build churches and monasteries. Church property was restored, the repair of churches from public funds was encouraged, and Christian clergy were exempted from taxation.

Constantine made it possible for many churches and monasteries to accumulate great wealth because it was now legal for them to receive grants and hold property and estates, which generated income. The churches and monasteries lavished most of this wealth on good works for the community.

It is unfortunate that there was no straightforward development of theological and spiritual values among those who embraced Christianity. Disputes plagued the course of history of the Egyptian church. While the most positive aspects of Christianity were being played out in the monastic movement, heresies within the church sadly threatened to undermine the essence of the faith. The differences arose on abstract issues concerning the nature of Jesus. Behind the disputes was the fact that the Christian ideal had come to a land of distinct and separate cultural traditions. Christianity attracted people from many backgrounds, with varying concepts of godliness and styles of worship. To define the new religion was, therefore, of crucial importance. The issue centered around definitions of such words as 'Father,' 'Son,' 'begotten,' and 'unbegotten.' If Jesus was both God and Man, had He two natures? If so, what was their relationship?

The chief protagonists were Arius, an elderly Alexandrian presbyter, and Alexander, the bishop of Alexandria. Arius held the view that "a time there was when He was not." In other words, that Jesus did not have the same nature as the Father, that He had been created in time, and was consequently not divine. Alexander believed that Father and Son were of one nature; that Jesus was both divine and human.

What is known as the Arian heresy was first denounced to the church of Alexandria by Melitius, bishop of Lycopolis (Asyut). When Melitius, however, later took it upon himself to ordain priests and consecrate bishops independently of Alexandria, thus creating a nationalistic movement in Upper

Egypt and challenging the authority of the bishop of Alexandria, this caused a further schism in the church. A need was now seen to officially define a dogma which would unify Christian belief and formulate the creeds of faith, and to settle dissensions in the church.

The Council of Nicea in 325 was one of the earliest and perhaps the most important of church councils. It was attended by the emperor Constantine and 310 bishops and their delegations from Egypt, Syria, Assyria, Asia Minor, Greece, and the West. The Syrian and Assyrian delegations included bishops from Antioch, Jerusalem, and Armenia. Goths and Romans represented the West. The leading sees were Alexandria and Antioch, the latter represented by the bishop Eustathius and the former by the bishop Alexander. Although Alexander officially led Egypt's delegation it was his deacon, Athanasius, who was his chief spokesman, and who brilliantly defended the orthodox faith. The Alexandrian delegation included not only Alexander and Athanasius, but Arius their antagonist, Melitius, and a large body of monks and hermits, many of whom bore disfigurements from Roman persecution. Both Potamon ('dedicated to Amon') the bishop of Hierakleopolis Magna (Ihnasya), and Paphnutius ('dedicated to his god'), from the Theban area, had had a right eye gouged out with a sword and the empty socket seared with a red-hot poker.

The Alexandrians, who had raised the issues which the council was to discuss, particularly on the nature of Christ, were the most argumentative of the representatives. In fact, considering the abstract nature of the dispute, it was discussed in an atmosphere both highly charged and antagonistic. The meeting started in dignity and solemnity but ended in an atmosphere of exasperation and antipathy. Each of the representatives was committed to his opinion and hostile to those of the others. From the moment the debate started, accusations were leveled and bandied around. The anger was perhaps not surprising in view of the fact that the council was held to settle questions that had already violently divided the church. The council was the consequence, not the cause, of religious dissension, and there were also personal jealousies and grievances in the air. The tall, dazzlingly attired emperor Constantine must have been sadly disillusioned with the Christian world torn by factions.

It says a great deal for the eloquence, reasoning, and persistence of Alexander's young deacon, Athanasius, that the Nicene Creed, to the effect that Father and Son are of the same nature, was finally sanctioned. Its twenty-one canons were worded by Alexander, Athanasius, and the bishop of Caesarea and approved and signed by the members of the council. This creed, which still retains a hold on the mass of Christendom, had a place in all Western liturgies at least until the end of the seventeenth century:

We believe in one God, the Father all-Sovereign, maker of all things, both visible and invisible: And in one Lord Jesus Christ, the Son of God, begotten of the Father, an only-begotten; that is, from the essence of the Father, God from God, Light from Light, true God from true God—begotten, not made—being of one essence with the Father; by whom all things were made, both things in heaven and things on earth; who for us men and for our salvation came down and was made flesh,was made man, suffered, and rose again the third day, ascended into heaven, cometh to judge the quick and the dead: And in the Holy Spirit.

(Translation from Gwatkin, H.M., in *The Cambridge Medieval History*, Vol. I, pp. 121–22).

Constantine formally received the decision of the bishops and issued a decree of banishment against those who refused to subscribe to the Nicene Creed. Arius, denounced as a heretic, was banished, and his books were burned. Melitius was allowed to retain his title and rank in Asyut, but not to ordain; those already ordained by him could resume their functions after a second ordination, and take their places below those ordained by the bishop of Alexandria.

Alexander and Athanasius returned to Egypt triumphant. Alexander emerged from the Arian controversy as the orthodox patriarch of Alexandria and a universally accepted doctor of the Christian church. Athanasius had established a bond between Alexandria and monasticism: as a result of his efforts, the monastic orders had been stamped with ecclesiastical approval at the Council of Nicea. When

Alexander died soon afterwards, Athanasius succeeded to the vacant see.

The historical appearance of Athanasius (c.293–373) is well documented. Alexander, the bishop of Alexandria, was entertaining the clergy in his home overlooking the sea-front, while a group of children were playing on the shore. They seemed to be enacting a religious ceremony, so Alexander sent for them and asked what game they were playing. They finally admitted that they had been imitating the sacrament of baptism. The one boy, Athanasius, who had enacted the role of bishop recited all the proper questions and rituals he had performed; when Alexander realized that he had left none out in his addresses, and had dipped the boys in the sea, he declared that the baptism was valid and he personally confirmed them. It was then that the bishop took Athanasius under his charge and later made him deacon.

The ethnic origin of Athanasius is not clear. The fact that he was bilingual suggests Egyptian ancestry, because the Greeks seldom bothered to learn the Egyptian language. Although his name is Greek, it was, as already noted, common practice for educated Egyptians to adopt or give their sons Greek names, just as they adopted Greek names for their cities and their gods and goddesses. Athanasius was small in stature, wore a short beard, and had light auburn hair, which is a characteristic found on many Egyptian mummies. Although this description might be compatible with a pure Egyptian descent, the argument is inconclusive. More persuasive perhaps are the facts that Athanasius spoke the Egyptian vernacular, sympathized with Egyptian sentiments, understood the Egyptian people, and was ardently nationalistic. He was a close friend and biographer of Saint Antony, with whom he communicated in Egyptian, since Antony was not bilingual. Later, when Athanasius was driven into exile he sought refuge among the Desert Fathers.

Theological disputes that were to split the church started soon after the Council of Nicea and the success of the Alexandrian delegation. Melitius, at one time critical of the Arians, now sided with them against Athanasius. He had strong backing in Upper Egypt. Although later convicted as an Arian and a heretic, Melitius was an ardent nationalist and must be listed among those who fought for Coptic Christianity. Indeed, as already mentioned, it was he who originally brought the Arian heresy to the attention of the bishop of Alexandria.

The supremacy of the Alexandrian church suffered its first blow when the bishop of Antioch founded a school in imitation of that of Alexandria. The second blow came three years later when the emperor Constantine founded a new capital. He chose the ancient Greek town of Byzantium, which became Constantinople ('Constantine's city') and was to gain the importance and prestige that had once belonged to Alexandria. It was embellished with great monuments that were shipped there from many ancient cities, including an Egyptian obelisk over thirty meters high. Constantinople, known as New Rome, became a new metropolis of Greek art and science as well as a refuge of Christian and secular learning. Although Alexandria rivaled the new eastern capital for another three centuries, its reputation as the seat of learning, which it had held since Ptolemaic times, had been undermined.

The see of Alexandria faced its greatest setback when the Arian leaders were recalled from banishment at the entreaty of the emperor's daughter Constantia. Constantine's successor, Constantius, also favored the Arians. He deposed Athanasius, set his followers to flee at the point of the sword, and placed his own bishop, Georgius, on the throne of the see of Alexandria. Thus began an era when ecclesiastical dignitaries excommunicated one another, and mobs sacked churches of opposing factions. Athanasius was driven into exile five times between 336 and 373, and his periods of exile coincided with the appointment of Arian bishops in Alexandria. Athanasius sought shelter with hermits in their isolated caves. He lived with Saint Antony near the Red Sea, and he also lived in the monastery in Kharga oasis for many years. During his exiles he successfully reconciled remaining differences between the monks and the hermits, some of whom did not want to join the monastic order, preferring their loosely cenobitic communities.

Archaeological evidence shows that there was a radical break in burial customs in Egypt in the fourth century. Throughout the third century, people continued to be buried in a manner that had become fashionable since the beginning of the first century, when a painted portrait panel of the deceased was inserted in the mummy wrappings. It was placed over the face of the mummy, and the shrouds and *cartonnage* were painted with scenes drawn from the traditional mortuary texts. In the fourth century, however, bodies began to be wrapped in the garments of daily life, or in tapestries that might have been used in homes. These bore no references to the ancient gods, not even conventional prayers to Osiris. This fact can only be explained as the loss of belief in the efficacy of age-old rituals with the spread of Christianity.

Byzantine Period

Political unrest continued. Under Theodosius I (375–395) Christianity was formally proclaimed the religion of the empire, the Arians were again declared heretical, and all forms of pagan cult were expressly forbidden on the threat of being charged with treason. At the death of Theodosius there was a formal partition of the empire between the emperor Honorius in Rome and the emperor Arcadius in Constantinople. Egypt fell under the jurisdiction of the latter. Theophilus, patriarch of Alexandria, displayed tremendous zeal in destroying ancient Egyptian temples. A wave of destruction swept over the land of Egypt. Tombs were ravaged, walls of ancient monuments scraped, and statues toppled. The famous statue of Serapis in Alexandria was burned and the Serapeum destroyed. It was a folly of fanaticism in the name of orthodoxy not, ironically, so different from that which had earlier oppressed Christianity in Rome.

The whole of the New Testament was translated into Coptic at this time (only the Psalms and selected writings had been translated before). The canon of the Coptic Bible is largely the same as the modern canon known in the West; it does, however, include part of the Book of Revelation which is not in the Greek Orthodox canon. The translators used a more colloquial form of their language than that used by demotic scribes, thus making their writings—biblical, theological, and liturgical—available to many more Egyptians. They chose the Egyptian word *neter* to describe God. It survived in Coptic as *nute*, but the specific meaning of the word, both its original in ancient Egyptian and its Coptic derivative, has been lost. Generations of scholars have deliberated over the actual meaning of the word and are even today not in agreement on its definition. Suffice it to say that the ancient Egyptians used both the singular *neter* and the plural *neteru* side by side in their mortuary texts, and that the Copts chose the singular form because, presumably, there was no other word that so aptly conveyed to their minds the conception of an active force—commanding, guiding, inspiring, and ordaining man's destiny.

During the fourth and fifth centuries many ancient temples were converted into monastic centers. Deir (monastery) al Madina and Deir al Bahari on the Theban necropolis are two well-known examples. Churches were also built in great number inside the chambers of ancient temples. For example, the second court of the mortuary temple of Ramses III at Madinet Habu was converted into a church, its wall reliefs covered with clay, plastered in stucco, and painted with Christian themes. And one of the earliest Christian buildings in Egypt was constructed between the birth-house and the coronation-house of the temple of Hathor at Dendera; some of the blocks from the birth-house were reused in the church's construction. It is possible that this church marked a famous Christian center of the fourth century, for Saint Jerome described an assembly of fifty thousand monks who celebrated Easter somewhere in the neighborhood of Dendera.

Pilgrims came from all over the Christian world to visit the monasteries in Egypt, especially the healing center of Saint Menas in the once fertile region of Maryut; they took home with them clay ampoules containing oil from the lamp that burned before the tomb of the saint. Rufinus, 380–401, in his ecclesiastical history, described a meeting of ten thousand monks at Arsinoë (ancient Crocodilopolis) in the Fayoum. This figure was repeated by Palladius, the historian of fourth century monasticism; in his *Historia Lausiaca*, which is a personal account of the lives of Egyptian monks during the height of the ascetic movement, he recorded that there were also twelve convents for women at Arsinoë. The bishop of Bahnasa estimated the number of monks in Middle Egypt at ten thousand, and nuns at twenty thousand, living in forty monasteries and convents. Archaeological evidence has revealed a huge monastic settlement in distant Kharga oasis, in the western desert, dating from the fourth century. Its necropolis of Bagawat (see p.139) contains over two hundred chapels. Wadi al Natrun once had fifty monasteries and over five thousand monks. East of Wadi al Natrun, at Kellia, there are about 750 abandoned hermitages dating to around the fifth century. This site was described in many early Christian writings such as those of Palladius and Rufinus.

As with most great movements that spread beyond the borders of the country in which they took root, contradictory traditions of the origins of monasticism have emerged. Western tradition credits Saint Paul, who lived around the middle of the third century, with being the first hermit, largely as a result of his *Life* written by Saint Jerome in the fourth century, and because he was older than the much more famous Saint Antony. Copts, however, do not regard Saint Paul's ascetic ideal as atypical of the period in which he lived. They look to Saint Antony, whose fame spread as a result of his biography written after his death (around 350) by Athanasius, as founder of the monastic movement and the prototype of the Egyptian monk. And they honor Saints Pachom and Shenuda as creators of disciplined, cenobitic monastic communities.

The Christian ideal could, therefore, be said to have been acted out in different modes of behavior throughout Egypt— from the ordinary Christian laity to the solitary recluse, from the urban priest to the cloistered nun, from sprawling monastic communities like those of Wadi al Natrun and Bagawat to the walled Pachomian monasteries. Although some pagan elements continued, these were curbed as much as possible. The Hermetic literature, hitherto regarded positively by the early church fathers, was now forbidden to Christians as it included magic; the texts were 'hermetically' sealed.

In Alexandria, factional disputes continued and there was a bitter struggle between the patriarchs of Alexandria on the one hand and those of Constantinople on the other. The Council of Constantinople, convened in 381, marked the final defeat of Arianism and had far-reaching effects for Egypt, for while adding a clause to the Nicene Creed affirming the divinity of the Holy Spirit, it declared that the bishop of Constantinople stood second only to the bishop of Rome. The council thus officially undermined the primacy of Alexandria. The riots that resulted in Alexandria were so violent that the Catechetical School, which had remained a force in the intellectual life of the city for nearly two centuries, was destroyed. The patriarchs of Alexandria fought to maintain their position in relation to Constantinople, but the breach had become too wide. Egypt's opposition to the Melkites, or 'Emperor's men,' representing Constantinople, became the latest episode in a long struggle for independence that was political as well as religious. The church had, unfortunately, become the medium through which differences that had long existed were loudly voiced.

Such differences were by no means confined to Egypt. The Nestorian heresy takes its name from Nestorius, the bishop of Constantinople, who declared that Christ's nature was humanity, into which divinity came. At the third church council at Ephesus, convened in 431, Nestorius was condemned and excommunicated. The church of Constantinople meanwhile has remained dyophysite, arguing that Christ's nature was in equal measure human and divine, with the two separate elements joined to form a perfect unity.

Foundation of the Coptic Orthodox Church

The Council of Chalcedon in 451 signaled Byzantine determination to exert authority in Egypt, and Egypt's equal determination not to submit to pressure. Ostensibly the point at issue was one of doctrine. The Egyptian church was 'monophysite' and laid its emphasis on the single nature of Christ, partly human and partly divine but indivisible. When a new statement of dogma at the Council of Chalcedon declared that Christ had two distinct natures 'concurring' in one person, this was unacceptable to Coptic orthodoxy. Although the creed of the earlier Council of Nicea formulated by Athanasius was left largely unchanged, there were minor amendments that included a clause opening the way to the possibility of future additions. The Nicene Creed in its revised form was accepted by the Byzantine church, but the Egyptians, the monophysites, would not compromise. Their refusal to endorse the revisionist doctrine eventually led to the separation of the Egyptian from both the Byzantine and the Western (Latin) churches forever.

There is little doubt that the precedence of the see of Constantinople over the see of Alexandria, which was ratified at the Council of Chalcedon, had something to do with Egypt's refusal to accept any doctrinal modification. After the Council of Chalcedon, the way was paved for the Coptic church to establish itself as a separate entity. The main center of learning for the Coptic church forthwith became the monastery of Saint Macarius in Wadi al Natrun. No longer even spiritually linked with Constantinople, theologians began to write more in Coptic and less in Greek. Coptic art developed its own national character, and the Copts stood united against the imperial power.

End of Byzantine Rule

For over 150 years there had been periods of peace and oppression under the rule of the Byzantine emperors. But, by the reign of Justinian (527–565), the Egyptian monophysites far outnumbered the opposing Melkite party in Egypt and refused to be coerced by them. Justinian tried drastic measures, imprisoning monophysites in the fortress of Babylon, but all this succeeded in doing was to aggravate the differences between the two groups. In fact, it completed the alienation of the Copts, who henceforward simply ignored any ecclesiastical representatives from Constantinople. They formally seceded from Byzantium, appointed their own patriarch of Alexandria (residing in Wadi al Natrun), and followed their own interpretation of the Scriptures. Egypt henceforth had two patriarchs of Alexandria, one upholding the monophysite beliefs of the majority of Egyptian Christians, the other rallying behind Constantinople.

In the fifth and sixth centuries when both the church of Constantinople, with its Greek adherents in Alexandria, and the Western church of Rome basked in the glory of imperial favor, accumulated great endowments, built splendid churches, and elaborated the ceremonial of worship, the Coptic clergy had to stint to survive. Nevertheless, these centuries saw a remarkable national revival in art, a spirit manifested in media such as wood, ivory, brass, copper, textiles, painting, and sculpture. The Coptic church, a remarkable monument of Christian antiquity, could look back with great pride to the age when its authority was acknowledged by all Christian sees.

Arab Conquest of Egypt

When Egypt was conquered by the Arabs in A.D. 641, the Copts, deeply hostile to Byzantine rule, gave support to the conquerors. During the siege of Babylon (Old Cairo) the Muslims camped to the north of the Roman fortress, and it was here that Amr ibn al As founded Fustat, a garrison city for the internal control of the Nile Valley. As capital of Egypt and seat of the government, the city rapidly increased in size and importance.

The Arabs were at first somewhat indifferent to the Copts. They were not yet interested in converting the people to Islam, which they still viewed as a purely Arab religion. Under the original treaty of surrender, security was guaranteed to the Copts, who were granted freedom of worship on condition they paid a poll tax. They were treated with benevolence, used for administrative purposes, allowed to repair or rebuild their churches, but were barred from military service.

As Fustat was slowly transformed from a military base into the administrative and commercial capital of the Arab province of Egypt, the conquerors came to depend more and more on the local population for food, raw materials, and clerical assistance. Copts were also employed in the fields of architecture, sculpture, painting, and crafts. With such increased contact, Arabic began to replace Greek as the language of government, culture, and commerce in the city, and in time filtered down to the rural population. As early as the twelfth century the patriarch Gabriel II admonished priests to explain the Lord's Prayer in vernacular Arabic, which would indicate on the one hand that there was a growing command of Arabic among the people and on the other that the Coptic language was not now widely understood. In the thirteenth and fourteenth centuries liturgical books began to carry Arabic translations alongside the Coptic, and there is little doubt that the bulk of the population was Arabic-speaking by this time.

The religious life of the Copts suffered relatively little after the Arab conquest, as evidenced by the continuity of the Coptic arts in monastic centers throughout the land and in Old Cairo. The Hanging Church (al Muallaqa, see p.83), for example, probably dates from the end of the seventh century, as does the church of Saint Barbara (see p.86). But increased taxation on non-Muslims and prohibitive fees for the right to construct or rebuild churches eventually evoked resentment, and there were insurrections in the eighth century on the part of some of the Copts which, by their failure, increased the prestige of the Arabs among others. The Muslim rulers took advantage of the iconoclastic war in Byzantium in the eighth and ninth centuries to ban the use of the human figure in art and to give permission for the destruction of images in churches. The result was that many Coptic paintings and frescoes were destroyed.

The conversion of the Copts to Islam was slow. Although the majority of Copts continued to practice their faith, and express it in artistic forms that came in irregular, but consistent, waves of creativity, the financial pressure was great. Up to the beginning of the eighth century, monasteries were exempted from taxes, but when these were enforced, along with severe penalties for non-payment, more Copts accepted the Islamic faith. By the ninth century, Islam had gained predominance in Egypt. The Copts were still allowed freedom of worship— religious coexistence was, in fact, only temporarily interrupted by the violent persecutions of al Hakim, regarded by many as mad. He destroyed churches and monasteries and severely persecuted Christians between 1012 and 1015. His successor al Zahir, however, showed renewed tolerance, and even permitted Copts who had been forced to accept Islam to return to their Christian faith.

In the Fatimid period, 969–1171, Muslim Egypt enjoyed a great era of prosperity, and the Coptic church generally flourished. The Melkite patriarch in Alexandria had gone back to Constantinople, and the Coptic patriarchate was moved from Wadi al Natrun to Cairo. The sympathetic attitude of the Fatimids towards the Copts was expressed in, among other things, their employment of Copts in the government, and their own participation in Christian feasts. But more significant, perhaps, is the reconstruction and adornment of churches and monasteries in Fatimid times. Having assimilated new themes and motifs from Syria and Constantinople, Coptic artists adopted or reinterpreted these, and new heights in Coptic artistic expression were reached, especially in the monastic centers in Middle and Upper Egypt.

Although the Copts continued to behave as loyal subjects when the Crusaders challenged the supremacy of Islam there was, understandably, some erosion of goodwill, and by the time Salah al Din founded the Ayyubid dynasty in the twelfth century the situation had subtly changed. Few churches were built or decorated, although crafts such as weaving and woodwork maintained their high standards. During the thirteenth century there was a brief spiritual revival among the Copts, though its impact on the church was hardly noticeable. Artistic expression seemed drained of its strength and there were no new avenues of expression.

With the coming of the Mamluks in 1250, Christianity in Egypt rapidly declined until, by the fourteenth century, Copts had become a small minority. Coptic history, as recorded by Coptic rather than Muslim historians and travelers, came to an end. The picture gained from a study of the monastic sites may in some measure reflect the general conditions of the Coptic church in medieval times. There were periods during which the monasteries were plundered and destroyed by marauding Bedouins, but they were rebuilt and reopened. The monasteries of Wadi al Natrun suffered at least three such devastations, and although they were restored, it is clear that artistic expression had declined sadly and lost a great deal of its former spiritual vitality. In fact the monastic center of Wadi al Natrun, and the monasteries of Saints Paul and Antony on the Red Sea coast, show large-scale borrowing from Byzantine and Syrian models. Many of the artists were themselves imported. Ibrahim al Nassikh al Baghdadi, from Iraq, was a famous iconographer in Egypt, as were Yuhanna the Armenian and Astasy al Rumi, the Greek, whose icons hang in many of the ancient churches of Old Cairo. There was little original work. Even panel paintings and miniatures were done by copyists.

Modern Revival

Not until the middle of the nineteenth century, under the leadership of the great reformer, educator, and statesman Pope Cyril (Kirollos) IV, did the Copts regain a sense of prestige and position. By then it was an upward path. One of the most important moves took place in the twentieth century, when the Higher Institute for Coptic Studies was founded in 1954. An extension of the Theological College, it was an attempt to restore a sense of religious identity and to promote and preserve the Coptic artistic heritage. In an attempt to rediscover the spiritual and artistic roots of Coptic Christianity in ancient Egypt, the revival has turned for inspiration to Egypt's ancient past.

Under the enlightened leadership and spirituality ushered in by Kirollos VI in 1959, the Coptic church also entered into ecumenical dialogues and took its place on boards and committees of the World Council of Churches. During his patriarchate, Kirollos laid the foundation stone for the construction of the monastery of Saint Menas on the historic site of Maryut; negotiated the translation of the relics of Saint Mark the Evangelist from Venice to Cairo in June 1968; and set in motion a program of building churches, crowned by the construction and inauguration of the new cathedral of Saint Mark in Cairo.

In October 1971, following the death of Kirollos VI seven months earlier, Shenuda III was elected to take his place at the head of the Coptic church as Pope and Patriarch of Alexandria and all Africa.

2

COPTIC CHRISTIANITY TODAY

The Copts, Orthodox Egyptian Christians, though a minority within an Islamic country, number over seven million in a total population of fifty million. Apart from some quarters in Cairo—including Shubra, Abbassia and al Daher—and the Delta city of Tanta, they are most strongly represented in Middle and Upper Egypt: Minya, Asyut, Akhmim, Girga, Nagada, Quft, Luxor, and Esna.

The spiritual leader of the Coptic community is Pope Shenuda III. Born in 1923, and regarded as the 117th successor of Saint Mark, Pope Shenuda has pursued both an ascetic and a scholarly life. He joined the monastery of Saint Mary (known as the monastery of the Syrians, *Deir al Suryan*) at Wadi al Natrun in 1954, and subsequently lived as a hermit in several monastic centers in the western desert. Pope Shenuda eventually returned to the monastery of the Syrians where, in 1962, he was ordained Bishop of Higher Theological Studies. The author of several books and a large number of articles on spirituality and theology, Pope Shenuda also takes a special interest in social services for the community, especially in the Sunday school movement.

Today there are about 105 Coptic Orthodox churches in Cairo, and some 150 Coptic institutions, including schools, orphanages, old age homes, hospitals, and social service centers. The number in rural areas is also rapidly increasing. The new cathedral of Saint Mark off Ramses Street in Cairo is the pride of the Coptic community. It has a seating capacity of five thousand, and the patriarchal library and residence are located there. The cathedral was founded in 1965 on the

44

occasion of the 1900th anniversary of the martyrdom of Saint
Mark. The body of Saint Mark originally reposed in the
church of Saint Mark in Alexandria but, around the year 828,
two merchants removed the relics to Venice, where the famous
cathedral of Saint Mark was erected in 883. According to
tradition, the head of the evangelist remained in Egypt,
variously reported as being carried to Wadi al Natrun, Cairo,
or Alexandria. Copts claim that today it rests in an ebony box
in the crypt beneath the altar of the cathedral of Saint Mark
in Alexandria, which was reconstructed in 1952.

Language

The Coptic language is the direct line of communication with
the past. Even when totally eclipsed as a spoken language by
Arabic (possibly as late as the seventeenth century) it
survived in some vernacular Arabic forms, such as the names of
the Coptic months, which are derived from the names of
ancient Egyptian gods: *Tut*, for example, from Thoth; *Hatur*
from Hathor. The dialect used in present-day church liturgies
is *Bohairic*, which was adopted when the monastery of Saint
Macarius (Abu Maqar) in Wadi al Natrun became the official
residence of the patriarch. Linguists have observed, however,
that the ancient language comprised several local dialects,
including *Sahidic* in Upper Egypt, *Fayumic* in the area of the
Fayoum, *Akhmimic* around Akhmim, and the closely related
'Middle Egyptian' dialect. Coptic is today being revived as a
written language, and is being taught in Sunday schools, but is
still bound to church rituals.

Music

Coptic music is vocal. Hymns, with no trace of musical
notation, were composed in the style of popular songs. In fact,
in common with the Greek Orthodox church, instrumental
music may not be used as an accompaniment to hymns; only the
clashing of cymbals and the striking of metal triangles are
permitted. Demetrius of Phalaron, the librarian in
Alexandria in 297 B.C., told of ceremonies in honor of Egyptian
gods using seven Greek vowels to produce harmonious sounds,
thus eliminating the need for instrumental accompaniment. To

this day these same seven vowels are chanted in Coptic hymns.

Church Services

Seven being a sacred number, Copts, like other Christians, also observe seven canonical sacraments: baptism, confirmation, eucharist, penance, orders, matrimony, and unction of the sick. A child is usually baptized within six weeks of birth by immersion in water three times. Confirmation is simultaneous with the act of baptism. In common with the Roman Catholic practice, the Copts require that the water be specially consecrated.

During services in a Coptic church, members of the congregation are segregated, males to the left and females to the right. Women are not obliged to cover their heads but they may not, under any circumstances, pass beyond the barrier, the transept, between the nave and the altar. Men, if they do so, observe the custom of first removing their shoes before stepping on the holy ground around the altar. On entering a church members of the congregation usually cross themselves, kneel before the altar, and pay homage to the icons of saints and the Holy Virgin on the walls.

A sense of awe and mysticism surrounds the sacerdotal functions in a Coptic church, which largely take place in the holy inner chambers out of sight of the congregation. Apart from eucharistic vessels, the Copts use five basic instruments: the chalice, a ritual goblet with a small, almost straight-sided conical bowl and a long stem ending in a round knob and a circular foot; the paten, a flat, circular dish with a vertical raised rim; the dome, which is placed over the consecrated bread in the middle of the paten; the spoon for administering communion; and the altar-casket, a small cubical box, the top of which has a circular opening large enough to admit the chalice. In Coptic tradition the eucharistic loaf, leavened bread freshly baked according to specific rituals, is customarily broken into small pieces and given before the holy wine. When not conducting a service, the priest comes among the people to bless them; and there is a reverence for sacred acts performed by children, especially young boys spreading incense, usually from metal censers.

It would require a separate volume to enumerate the religious customs of a people so pious and so much given to ceremony as the Copts. The most important celebrations, as in the early church, are Palm Sunday and Holy Week leading to Easter. That is to say, Easter (the Resurrection) is more important to the Copts than Christmas (the Birth of Christ). The other important celebration is the feast of Epiphany, which consists of a blessing with consecrated water for the whole community, performed by the bishop or patriarch in full pontifical apparel.

Easter

For Egypt's Orthodox Christians, Easter is a grand religious celebration. It usually falls several weeks after that observed by Western Christians, and is a tradition that has long endured on the banks of the Nile. Copts prepare for Easter by fasting for fifty-five days. During this extended period no animal products—meat, eggs, milk, fish—are consumed. Cereals and foods of plant origin form the main diet, particularly vegetables cooked in olive oil. Neither coffee nor wine is taken and, moreover, no food or drink whatsoever should be consumed between sunrise and sunset. As with the Muslim Ramadan, dispensation is granted in cases of illness or weakness.

Holy Week (*Isbu' al Alam*, 'Week of Pain') is a week of prayer, when specific events in the last week in the life of Jesus are commemorated. It starts with a mass on Palm Sunday (*Hadd al Za'f*), at which a priest or bishop blesses fronds of a palm tree. As in the early church, a procession forms with the clergy bearing the cross, incense tapers, and palm fronds, and moves around the church, praying at each altar, the principal icons, and the reliquaries. On Palm Sunday Copts remember also their own dear departed. They visit family graves and place palm fronds and bunches of flowers around the tombs. Palm fronds are woven into crosses, frequently exquisitely designed with rosaries fashioned into the weave, and these are hung on the front doors of houses or inside the sitting room. Sometimes the fronds are made into intricate designs of angels' wings. They are sold at street corners near churches throughout the country, but especially in Old Cairo.

The following Friday is Good Friday (*al Goma' al Hazina*, 'Sad Friday'), when church altars are draped in black, and this is followed by *Sabt al Nur*, 'Saturday of Light,' so named for the miraculous light that appeared in the church of the Holy Sepulcher in Jerusalem. A candlelight procession takes place through the streets at dawn, in memory of the entry of Jesus into Jerusalem.

Throughout Holy Week, children are busy painting hard-boiled eggs in bright colors. Grocery stores stock up with the necessary dyes, and shops display a wide variety of traditional chocolate Easter eggs. On the evening before Easter, the service of thanksgiving starts at about seven o'clock and goes on until midnight. The priest is robed in full ecclesiastical attire with stole and crown, and the assisting clergy form a semicircle around him as he stands in front of the elaborately adorned sanctuary screen. Young boys in long white robes assist in the service. Special prayers are said for the troubled and ailing, for the River Nile, and for the fruits of the earth. The opening of the door of the sanctuary to reveal the holy inner chambers with the altar is an act that symbolizes the rolling away of the stone from the tomb where Jesus was buried. The priest and the clergy forthwith raise their crosses and banners high in jubilation, and process round the church, intoning a joyous hymn.

Holy Communion follows. Members of the congregation first shake hands, symbolizing fellowship, and then line up, men and women separately, to receive the eucharist: seven loaves of freshly baked bread, made of the finest wheat flour, baked in a special oven by a member of the church, are offered to the priest. He carefully inspects each to select the perfect one, as it represents the faultlessness of Jesus. The loaf must never, according to tradition, be cut with a knife but should always be broken by hand in a special manner. The pieces are dipped in the holy wine (unfermented wine, made by soaking dried grapes in water, without trampling by foot; it is distributed to churches in large wicker-covered jars). The eucharist is received standing, and afterwards the officiating priest consumes the balance of the wine and bread. He then moves along the aisle in a final blessing, and the congregation rises to leave the church, uttering such phrases as "Christ has risen" and "Indeed, He has risen." Some members of the congregation purchase sacred loaves as they leave. Like the eucharist, these are stamped with a cross at the center, representing Jesus, and with twelve small crosses representing the twelve disciples. The bread is taken home, either to be consumed later or to be placed beneath a pillow as a personal blessing.

Celebrations for Easter Sunday (*'Id al Qiyama*, 'Feast of the Resurrection') include a traditional lamb dish known as *fatta*, made of rice and *baladi* bread soaked in lamb broth, vinegar, and garlic. Hard-boiled eggs, peeled and fried to a golden brown, adorn this appetizing and filling dish, which is served with yogurt. It is followed by a shortbread pastry stuffed with dates and nuts and coated in sugar, a tasty combination known as *kahk*.

Easter is a time of alms-giving, part of an age-old tradition in the Nile Valley, when those of means help people less fortunate than themselves. It is also a time for good fellowship and, of course, merry-making by children. They walk along the streets, usually in groups, to show off their new clothes bought specially for the occasion. If old enough, they weave colored, crinkly paper into the spokes of their bicycles, or group together to hire a donkey-cart for a few hours. The sounds of singing and drum-beating fill the air as the carts travel along the main thoroughfares. In Cairo, they move along the Nile corniche, while public gardens and the Zoo are filled with holiday-makers. Easter is a long holiday weekend, and a popular one, because the next day, Monday, is *Shamm al Nesim*. This Egyptian national celebration of the first day of spring for both Christians and Muslims has its origins in ancient Egyptian festivals associated with the rebirth of the land.

Christmas

The Coptic Christmas is a much shorter holiday than Easter. It falls on January 7, and *al Laila al Kabira* (the 'Big Night,' Christmas Eve) on the 6th ends forty-three days of fasting, when no animal food is taken. A large meal is eaten after midnight, after a church service and midnight mass. Early on Christmas morning children go to church in new, brightly-colored clothes to light a candle and receive a blessing. For adults there is an exchange of visits. Most of the women stay at home throughout the day to welcome visitors, while the men schedule part of their time to pay visits to relatives and neighbors. During the last ten years, Western Christmas tradition has become more widespread in Egypt, in the sale of Christmas trees and baubles.

The Copts have seasons of fasting matched by no other Christian community. The great fast of fifty-five days before Easter and the fast of forty-three days before Christmas have already been mentioned. In addition, the three-day fast of Yunan (who stayed in the stomach of the whale for three days) falls between Epiphany and the great fast; the Fast of the Apostles (commemorating the martyrdom of Saints Peter and Paul), which is variable in length, begins fifty days after Easter and ends on July 12; and the fifteen-day fast in honor of the Assumption of the Virgin begins on August 7.

Weddings

Coptic weddings, which do not take place during the great fast before Easter, are surrounded by ritual. The betrothed couple, who may be as closely related as second cousins, are first formally engaged at a ceremony where rings are exchanged. Although it is a solemn contract, accompanied by readings and prayers, the engagement may be broken. The marriage service, however, is a final binding commitment. It usually takes place after about a year, during which time the couple gets to know one another (especially if the union has been arranged between the two families). This is when the dowry and the furnishings for their home are discussed by the families.

On the wedding day, the bride and bridegroom are escorted separately to the church. The bride wears a white wedding dress and veil and the church is decorated with candles, flowers, and sometimes ribbons connecting the pews. The service lasts for an hour or more, amidst incense and musical accompaniment. The bride and groom are anointed with oil on their wrists and foreheads, and crowns are briefly placed on their heads (a handkerchief for poorer families). There is usually a reception afterwards, which today is often a lavish affair at a private club or hotel, and then the couple either go on honeymoon or move directly into their new, fully-furnished home. A church service is not compulsory; a couple may be married by a priest in their own home, but it is the duty of the priest to make sure that both parties are acting of their own free will. Village weddings are similar, but are naturally more modest; after the church service the bride's furniture is ceremoniously transported from her father's house to her new home.

Divorce is not permitted in the Coptic church, except in extreme circumstances such as adultery, proved according to the civil law. It is, even then, a long and complicated procedure. In the event of a man converting to Islam in order to marry another woman, the wife may sue for divorce on grounds of bigamy.

Other Customs

Among Egyptians (Christians and Muslims alike) a sense of the supernatural remains strong. The Copts believe in miracles like visitations of the Holy Virgin, whose apparitions were sighted in the Cairo suburbs of Zeitun in 1968 and Shubra in 1986. Copts also believe in the efficacy of sacred charms for protection, especially against the evil eye—the casting of a covetous look to cause grievous harm—and evil spirits. They frequently entreat holy men, priests or sheikhs, to exorcise these spirits on their behalf. The belief in the power of patron saints is extremely strong in Egypt. If, among the poor, prayers to God are of no avail, both Christians and Muslims may ask a scribe to write a letter to a specific saint with pleas as varied as curing the sick and solving personal problems. These letters are not signed because, as in ancient times when letters addressed to the dead or to local deities were written by scribes, it is taken for granted that the holy saint knows who has written them.

It is interesting to note that Egyptians still observe some traditions that appear to have their origins in the remote past. This is especially apparent in the rituals surrounding death. A funeral service is held in church, prayers are offered at the tomb and, on the third day, special prayers are held in the home. Mourning is observed for forty days, during which time the home is open for visits of condolence. On the fortieth day, a special memorial service is held in church. The timing of this service might be related to the fact that it took a minimum of forty days (and up to seventy) to complete the mummification of the deceased in ancient times. That /is to say, there was a similar period of mourning. Also, when Egyptians place flowers at the graves of the dead in annual remembrance and on important religious holidays, food is taken and consumed; in ancient times, the food and drink placed on offering tables for the *ka*, or spirit of the deceased, was regarded as specially blessed, and was eaten.

Pilgrimages

There is a strong and persistent tradition that supports the Bible story (Matt. 2:13–15) of the Flight into Egypt. It is a tradition shared by Christians and Muslims (who regard Jesus as a prophet along with Abraham, Moses, and Muhammad). There are literally dozens of sites throughout the Delta and Middle Egypt that are regarded as holy, and to which people make pilgrimage because they are places where the Holy Family visited, rested, or took refreshment during their sojourn. At Bahnasa in Middle Egypt, for example, near the site of the ancient city of Oxyrhynchus, which was an episcopal see in the fifth century, Coptic tradition holds that the Family traveled there on an ass and attracted those with infirmities, who received healing. Coptic and Muslim sources are not always in agreement on the route taken, nor on the duration of the visit—Copts believe that the Holy Family remained in Egypt for a little over three and a half years, while Muslim traditions have seven years—but such differences only serve to strengthen the tradition.

Among the sites that enjoy popularity as places where the Holy Family rested are the towns of Bubastis (Tell Basta), Bilbeis, Samannud, and Sakha in the Delta, where annual pilgrimages are made. Babylon (Old Cairo) and the church of the Holy Virgin on the banks of the Nile at Maadi, a suburb south of Cairo, are also hallowed sites. The latter is believed to mark the point where the Family embarked by boat for Upper Egypt. Mataria (ancient Heliopolis) enjoys great popularity as the place where the Virgin rested beneath a tree, refreshed herself, and washed the clothes of the Child

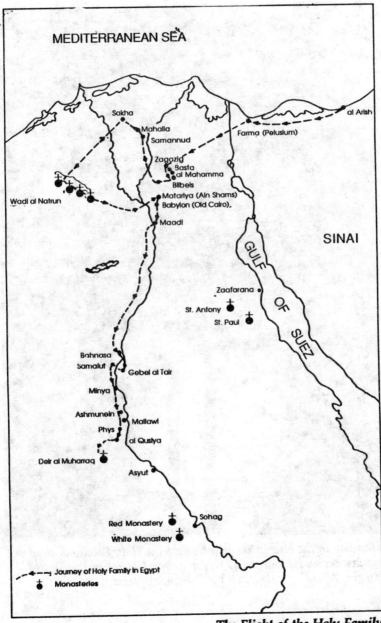

The Flight of the Holy Family

Stairway to the Nile at the point where the Holy Family is supposed to have begun its journey to Upper Egypt. Church of the Blessed Virgin, Maadi. Photograph by Cassandra Vivian.

in the spring. (What is today known as the 'Virgin's Tree'. at Mataria grew from the shoot of a sycamore that was planted in 1672 and fell on June 14, 1906. According to a medieval Arab writer, the original tree was a balsam.)

Many towns have a *mulid* or annual festival in honor of the Virgin. One of the most important is the pilgrimage on August 22 to Gebel al Tair ('Mount of Birds'), on the east bank of the Nile almost opposite Samalut in Middle Egypt. This, according to tradition, is the site where Mary feared for the safety of Jesus because a large rock threatened to fall on their boat from the mountain overlooking the river. But Jesus extended His hand and prevented its falling. His imprint remained on the rock, and the church of the Lady of the Palm was built in commemoration of the event.

The pilgrimage at Gebel al Tair starts on the western bank of the Nile. Young and old, rich and poor travel from neighboring villages and, indeed, from distant provinces. They come by train, by donkey-cart, or on foot. Children are clad in gaily-colored clothes, often with bright head-scarves. They cross the river from Samalut on river craft assembled for the occasion, and join a convoy of vehicles of all kinds, filled with happy, laughing people, clapping, drumming, and singing. The pilgrims proceed from the banks of the Nile to the foot of the mountain, where they unload bedding, baskets of food, and even cooking equipment (such a pilgrimage is no short homage—the pilgrims have come for an extended visit) and then they start to climb.

At the top of Gebel al Tair is the church dedicated to the Holy Virgin and nearby, overlooking the Nile Valley, is an elegant resthouse that was completed in 1988 (pilgrims used to stake their territory by laying down mattresses, personal belongings, and provisions near the holy place). Today, the area has been organized for the ever-increasing numbers of pilgrims. Daily they enter the church, pass their hands across paintings of Mary and Jesus, and move their lips in silent prayer. The site enjoys great popularity because it is believed to have healing qualities.

Another site popularly associated with the Flight is the village of Durunka, some ten kilometers south of Asyut, where an important mulid is held each year. The monastery of Saint

Mary, Deir Durunka, like that of Gebel al Tair, is situated near the cliff face. The Holy Family are believed to have rested in one of the many caves here. Later, these same caves were inhabited by hermits. Today, to accommodate the thousands of pilgrims who make their way to Durunka, new buildings have been erected near the sacred site.

Another monastery of Saint Mary, known as Deir al Muharraq (the 'Burnt Monastery'), is the largest and wealthiest monastery in Middle Egypt. It is situated in the western desert north of Asyut, and is best approached from Qusiya. Medieval and modern historians and travelers alike have been consistent in describing the site as a place of healing, and during the great fast preceding Easter, huge crowds travel there to receive blessing from the monks, to have their children baptized, or to pray for a cure. Over fifty thousand people are estimated to make this annual pilgrimage.

The monks of Deir al Muharraq relate a long-standing tradition that the church of the Blessed Virgin within the walled complex, apart from being a traditional place of healing, was the first church to be built in Egypt. They claim that it was constructed after Saint Mark's arrival in Alexandria in the middle of the first century. The large church dedicated to Saint George was reconstructed in the nineteenth century, and the new church of the Holy Virgin was built in 1964. Both were damaged during a fire in 1988, and are being restored. This monastery is well known for its charitable work among villagers. Many of the monks in residence are graduates of Cairo and Alexandria Universities.

Saints and Martyrs

Pilgrimages are also made to tombs of saints and martyrs during mulids. These are joyous occasions, when the people are confident that their participation in the 'second birth' of the saint to a life everlasting will bring blessings on them.

One of the most popular such pilgrimages is to the monastery of Saint Dimiana, north of Mansura in the Delta. This saint (see p.26) was tortured and killed in the time of Diocletian along with forty other young girls. Her shrine has been incorporated into the newly reestablished diocese of

Damietta. The mulid in honor of Dimiana takes place in May. Pilgrims come from all parts of Egypt and pitch tents around the monastery, and they remain in the area for a period of not less than a week. Although the earliest of the four churches within the monastery of Saint Dimiana was destroyed by flooding, the western part of the second church, known as the Old Church, was built on top of what is believed to be the tomb of the saint, where her relics are housed. Three steps lead to the tomb, enclosed by a wooden screen to which pilgrims attach votive offerings or pieces of cloth torn from their handkerchiefs and clothing. Such offerings are made because Dimiana is honored for giving fruitfulness to women and long life to the children of women who have lost offspring at a tender age.

Saint Barsum the Naked (Barsum al Arian) is another venerated saint, who performed many miracles and died in 1317. His relics are in the church that bears his name in the village of Ma'sara, between Tora and Helwan, and his mulid takes place on September 27.

Three thousand six hundred Egyptian martyrs in the area of Esna refused to offer certificates of sacrifice to the gods in the reign of Decius (249–251), and the convent of the Holy Martyrs was built in their memory. Of the two churches within the enclosure wall, one is a twentieth-century construction dedicated to the Holy Virgin and the other, older church was built and dedicated to the martyrs in the year 786 but was reconstructed several times. In the older church are some icons that date to medieval times; they were made by pilgrims who came to the area to honor Saint Amon (Amonius), who was bishop of Esna at the beginning of the fourth century. To him is attributed the building of the original monastery.

The monastery of the Martyrs (Deir al Shuhada) in Akhmim is another important place of pilgrimage, and a site of not inconsiderable historic importance. The monastery is situated within the cemetry of Akhmim, and is the place where the Book of Proverbs (one of the earliest complete papyrus manuscripts of Christian literature in existence) was found. Indeed, the section known as the Proverbs of Solomon was translated into the Akhmimic dialect of Coptic in the fourth century.

Also in Akhmim is the convent of the Holy Virgin (Deir al Adra) which is approached from the canal that leads to the town of Hawawish. It is of somewhat late construction, dating to the late seventeenth century, and is the site of several annual celebrations, the most important of which is the Assumption of the Holy Virgin on August 22.

Social Services

Akhmim has long been known as an active and prosperous community. The Coptic social center at Hawawish provides opportunities for a wide array of activities ranging from health and child care to crafts and technical training. Akhmim's beautiful weaving and embroidery are well known and much sought after both in Egypt and abroad.

The large, multi-purpose community center at Beni Suef is one of the biggest and most well-run in Egypt. A daycare center has been set up for infants and young children of working mothers. Moreover, as a result of the tendency for working families today to have smaller homes with no room for aged parents, an old age home has been set up by the patriarchate of Beni Suef, staffed by young Egyptian women. There is also a daycare center for the aged, where food, reading matter, and television are provided on a daily basis. Such centers have become extremely popular, as they provide old people with opportunities to share recreation, news, and gossip.

The largest training center for such services is run by the diocese of Beni Suef in the village of Bani Bakhit. Another, for girls, is located in the beautiful town of Bayad al Nasara, about two kilometers north of Beni Suef. Here, the convent of the Holy Virgin (Deir al Adra) provides vocational training, which ranges from Sunday-school instruction to various trades and crafts. Under the guidance and with the encouragement of Bishop Athanasius of Beni Suef, the convent has become a retreat for the Coptic Order of the Daughters of Saint Mary, and there is also a training center for church deacons.

Monastic Revival

In recent years there has been a revival of the monastic movement in Egypt, in response to the continual growth in population, and probably to increased materialism that is manifested in urban areas. Monasteries and convents all over the country are being rebuilt, expanded, or renovated, and increasing numbers of youths are taking to the cloth. Today, there are over twenty-five functioning monastic sites in Egypt. Indeed, university graduates frequently choose to spend some time at a monastery before commencing their careers; there they gain spiritual enlightenment while at the same time contributing to the monastery by carrying out experiments in agriculture, animal husbandry, and related small industries.

Monasteries are to be found on the Mediterranean coast west of Alexandria, throughout the Delta, in Wadi al Natrun, in Old Cairo and the Cairo suburbs of Giza and Helwan, along the Red Sea coast, in the Fayoum, and throughout Middle and Upper Egypt (see *Chapter Six*).

Coptic Seminaries

The name of Abuna Daud, Father David, who later became known as the patriarch Kirollos IV, is linked with the opening of the first Coptic college in 1855, and that same year he opened three other schools in Cairo: one for girls in Azbakiya and two others, one for girls and one for boys, in Harat al Saqqayin. The first Coptic theological seminary was opened in 1893 in the Cairo suburb of Abbassia, and its conscientious program of study has resulted in consistently high standards.

In addition, the monastery of Saint Mercurius (Abu Seifein) at the village of Tamouh, some eleven kilometers south of Giza, has been used as a training center for church deacons since 1967, and a number of similar training centers are being planned all over the country.

The Coptic Catholic Theological Seminary in the Cairo suburb of Maadi dates to the beginning of the eighteenth century, when Franciscan and Jesuit missionaries brought their strict educational standards to Egypt, later starting theological training in seminaries in the Muski (old Cairo), Tanta, Minya, and other areas.

* * *

Today's Coptic youth are avidly interested in their heritage. They are a proud minority with a strong sense of national identity. Many young people spend their weekends in the churches of Old Cairo volunteering their expertise to interested visitors. As already mentioned, the Coptic language is being taught in Sunday schools. And each Friday night, thousands attend the assembly hall in the complex of the new cathedral of Saint Mark in Cairo to hear Pope Shenuda address them. He symbolizes their faith and their identity, combining the qualities of evangelist, ascetic, and administrator. Pope Shenuda is, moreover, a spiritual leader who preaches with elegance and eloquence.

3

COPTIC ART

Coptic art, the distinctive Christian art of Egypt, includes works of diverse character because there was no separation between 'art' and 'craft' in the early Christian era; the capital of a column and an illustrated manuscript were as much forms of creative expression as paintings and sculpture. From burial grounds come funerary stelae, or tombstones, cartonnage sarcophagi, and fragments of woven textiles from clothing in which the deceased were laid to rest. Monastic centers, churches, and shrines provide stone and wood carvings, metalwork, wall and panel paintings, as well as a wealth of utilitarian objects like ivory combs, wooden seals for impressing sacred bread, pottery, and glassware.

Coptic art owes a great debt to two main sources: the classical world and ancient Egypt. Objects made in Greek style, or under the direct influence of classical art, include stone carvings of Aphrodite, Leda, Hercules, winged victories, cupids bearing garlands, and the vine branches of Bacchus. Monuments of mixed Greek–Egyptian character are the relief slabs that were probably used as wall decorations in churches; they frequently feature pilasters surmounted by stylized Corinthian capitals, sphinxes, or fish. Finally, Egyptian influence is best seen in funerary stelae, which have survived in large number throughout Egypt. They are square or rectangular in shape, sometimes curved at the top, or with a triangular pediment. Many have a tiny square cavity, which penetrated to the back of the stela. Such cavities were common in ancient Egyptian cemeteries, and incense was burned in them in the belief that the spirit of the dead would enjoy its

61

perfume. In the early Christian era stelae were erected in pagan and Christian burial grounds and were usually inscribed in Greek or Coptic with the name and details of the life or titles of the deceased, and the day of death. The carvings on them included Greek–Egyptian motifs. A figure, for example, often robed like an aristocratic Greek, reclining on a bed and holding a drinking vessel or grapes, might be flanked by the jackal-god Anubis and the hawk-headed Horus.

The persistence of ancient Egyptian symbolism in early Christian art was once a controversial issue among religious historians who did not recognize evidence of 'pagan' inspiration in Christian art. Now, it is accepted that the ansate cross, the *ankh* or hieroglyphic sign for the word 'life,' was intentionally adopted by the early Christians. In fact, many relief slabs show both the ankh and the Christian cross together, frequently flanked by the first and last letters of the Greek alphabet, the alpha and omega, symbolizing Christ's completeness, being the beginning and the end of all things. Other examples of Egyptian symbolism in early Christian art are the Holy Spirit shown descending in the form of a winged bird, like the soul of the deceased, the *ba*, in ancient Egypt; the archangel Michael weighing souls in the balance, which is akin to the ancient Egyptian god of wisdom, Thoth, weighing the heart of the deceased in the scales of justice; and Saint George and the dragon, reminiscent of the god Horus spearing Set, often portrayed as an evil serpent.

In addition to the classical, Egyptian, and Greek–Egyptian heritages in Coptic art, there are also Persian, Byzantine, and Syrian influences. Egyptian master weavers and artists were attracted to Persia in the third century with the rise of the Sassanian kingdom before the founding of Constantinople. When they returned, a new Persian repertory of themes (such as opposing horsemen or two facing peacocks drinking out of the same vessel) was introduced to Egypt. Borrowing from one culture to another is a natural process of cultural growth. In the fourth century, when Christianity made a triumphal entry into the Roman world, the art forms of ascendant Byzantium spread to Egypt, and continued even after the Coptic church broke away from the Eastern Roman church, because Egypt remained, politically, a part of the Roman

Empire. The Copts, however, were disenchanted with Alexandria as the center of culture (despite it being the city of Saint Mark's martyrdom) because it was associated with the Byzantine church. They turned more towards the Holy Land, the birthplace of Jesus Christ; Syrian influence on Coptic art became apparent in the fifth century. And, as the more forceful, orientalized style penetrated Egypt, a certain rigidity came with it. Some motifs that made their way to Egypt from Syria were ultimately of Persian origin, including animals and birds in roundels, and griffins.

The integration of contrasting configurations—classical, Egyptian, Greek–Egyptian, and Persian pagan motifs, as well as Byzantine and Syrian Christian influences—led to a trend in Coptic art that is difficult to define, because it is not possible to trace a unity of style. Unfortunately, early collections of Christian art were made without recording details of the sites from which they came, making it virtually impossible to trace artistic development through time. There is no way to tell, for example, how long classical and Greek–Egyptian motifs continued after the adoption of Christianity as the state religion of the Roman Empire. All that can be said is that Coptic art is distinctive, and that it differs from that of Antioch, Constantinople, and Rome.

In studying the objects in the Coptic Museum in Cairo, as well as in the various monastic centers, it seems possible that sophisticated work was produced by highly talented craftsmen at the same time as work that is characterized by folk simplicity. This can be seen in ivory work, tapestries, paintings, and architectural decorations. It is tempting to link this dichotomy with the schism in religious beliefs between the Melkites, who enjoyed royal patronage, and the monophysites, who did not. But there is another possible, more plausible, explanation:

Egypt had a long tradition of master craftsmen of different trades who, throughout ancient history, worked under the direction of a supervisor and in turn oversaw the work of a group of apprentices. Sometimes a high priest (as in the Old Kingdom) or an 'Overseer of All the Works of the King' (New Kingdom), the supervisor could recognize inferior workmanship, correct drawings, and generally ensure the required standard, whatever that happened to be during different periods. If there were changes in theme or style, this could only be brought about on instruction from the supervisor, who was empowered to authorize the change. Naturally the master craftsman had experience in handling large groups of men. Throughout the period of Roman rule of Egypt, there was a tendency for such master craftsmen to move around the Roman Empire, gravitating towards the centers that could pay for their professional services. They worked in Alexandria and were summoned by the emperors to Rome and Constantinople. There they sculpted classically draped forms as competently as they had the stylized Egyptian, and they carved languid reclining figures with no less devotion.

Scholars are not in agreement over which works of art can safely be regarded as Alexandrine—that is to say, executed by Egyptian craftsmen in Alexandria. (Only a few can be safely attributed to Egypt through consideration of subject matter or style. They include a casket now in the museum in Wiesbaden that is sculpted with a sphinx and the allegory of Father Nile; a small box in the British Museum showing the squat, typically Coptic figure of Saint Menas in a niche; and three plaques from the side of Maximian's throne at Ravenna Museum that have been attributed by art historians to Egyptian carvers.) Also, when the Copts seceded from the Byzantine church, master craftsmen who had worked for Byzantine patrons continued to do so. They had mastered the technique of deeper drill carving and supervised the execution of works of great sophistication, (*vide* the stucco wall decorations to be found in the monastery of the Syrians at Wadi al Natrun and the friezes from Bawit in the Coptic Museum).

Meanwhile, however, monasteries and churches that were built in Upper Egypt, especially in the fifth and sixth centuries, were adorned with carvings and paintings that show an expression of faith that was highly personal, executed by craftsmen who were not controlled by a supervisor to maintain the standards. There was a breakdown in the apprenticeship system and, as a result, stone and wood friezes, painted panels, and ivory work were produced that were crude and depended for their appeal largely on qualities of design.

This is especially apparent in representations of human figures, which are of strange proportion, being somewhat squat with large heads. A convincing explanation for this has yet to be made. It has been suggested that Coptic artists were producing work in reaction to the realism of ancient Egyptian and Greek paganism and that this, too, is the reason why the early Christians did not encourage the production of statuary in the round. While the tendency seems, indeed, to have been a departure from Hellenistic Alexandrine tradition towards an abstract two-dimensional style, this may not necessarily have been calculated. Rather, it may be an example of free artistic expression: naive, unsophisticated, yet forceful.

Efforts have been made to classify Coptic art into epochs but this is somewhat artificial. While every culture has phases of cultural production, this is visible only when seen from an historical vantage. As E.R. Dodds comments, "The practice of chopping history into convenient lengths and calling them 'periods' or 'ages' has . . . drawbacks. Strictly speaking, there are no periods in history, only in historians; actual history is a smoothly flowing continuum, a day following a day." (*Pagan and Christian in an Age of Anxiety*, p.3)

This is true of art. Day by day, through the centuries of Ptolemaic rule, while Greek culture became inextricable from the ancient Egyptian, a national heritage yet remained. This apparent contradiction is best exemplified in the literature of the Late Period, in which such syncretistic compilations as the Hermetic texts (see *Introduction*) developed alongside a more or less consistent pattern of thought and behavior, as in the literature discussed in *Chapter One*. In art, the diverse influences resulted in an admixture of motifs. Yet, despite this, distinctive 'Egyptian' traits set Coptic art apart from any other. The movement was continuous, but not necessarily smooth.

No other early Christian movement has such an abundance of paintings of persons who received honor in their own country. Egypt's martyrs, saints, patriarchs, hermits, and ascetics, some of whom were honored throughout the Christian world, received special distinction in Egypt. Their heroic deeds, sufferings, or miracles were told in legend, their relics became the focus of worship and, in accordance with ancient traditions, places of healing. Sometimes, in ancient temples that were converted to chapels or churches, a row of venerated hermits, monks, and the founders of monasteries were depicted on walls plastered to cover rows of ancient Egyptian deities carved in relief.

The human figures, whether in paintings, carvings, or tapestries, are shown from the front with serene faces and idealized expressions. The outlined, almond-shaped eyes are strongly reminiscent of the painted wooden panels from Bawit and the Fayoum, dating to the first and second centuries, which were placed over the head of the deceased and bound into the mummy wrappings. These panels themselves resemble cartonnage sarcophagi of the late pharaonic period. In fact, the so-called Fayoum portraits, with the full face and large obsessive eyes—a feature of Roman medallions and much early Christian art—are now regarded by art historians as the prototypes for the Byzantine icons.

Jesus Christ was usually shown enthroned, surrounded by triumphant saints or angels, or blessing a figure beside Him. He was always depicted as King, never the suffering servant. Egypt was a land where leadership was idealized and kingship, both on earth and in the afterlife, was something the people understood. A triumphant Jesus—reborn, benevolent, and righteous—is one of the most significant and continuous characteristics of Coptic art. Another is that Egyptians did not delight in painting scenes of torture, death, or sinners in hell; in the few exceptions where a holy man is painted undergoing torture, it is implied rather than graphically depicted. This is in tune with ancient Egyptian artistic tradition which, in the words of Cyril Aldred, tended to "magnify only the heroic and beneficent qualities of divinities and kings, and not the horrific power of tyrants and demons." (*Egyptian Art in the Days of the Pharaohs*, p. 12)

The study of Coptic art and architecture was for too long a sadly neglected field. One of the reasons for this is that early archaeologists showed no interest in Christian antiquities. They regarded Coptic art as decadent, dull, and non-classical. It is astonishing to us today to note that Champollion (the French scholar who deciphered hieroglyphic writing from the famous Rosetta Stone), while carrying out excavations at

Madinet Habu on the Theban necropolis, discovered a fine
fifth-century church there but did not even mention it in his
official report. In places where ancient Egyptian temples had
been converted into churches and the walls plastered and
painted with Christian themes, these layers were removed as
just so much debris obscuring the ancient Egyptian reliefs
below. No effort was made to photograph the wall paintings
before removal, or to record any architectural features. Vital
evidence was consequently lost from numerous temples
including Deir al Bahari, Madinet Habu, and Karnak at
Luxor, and those of Dendera and Edfu.

The first person to realize the value of Coptic art and make
an effort to preserve it was the French scholar Gaston
Maspero. In 1881, in his capacity as director of the Egyptian
Antiquities Service (now Antiquities Organization), he set
aside one of the halls of the Museum of Antiquities, then in
the suburb of Bulaq, for the first collection of Coptic art. His
encouragement of Egyptologists to undertake serious
excavation resulted in the preservation of the remains of the
monastery of Saint Apollo in Bawit (west of Dairut in Middle
Egypt) and of the monastery of Saint Jeremias on the Sakkara
plateau. Several scholars published descriptions of Coptic
churches, carvings, and crafts, but professional emphasis on
dated material, and the fact that no churches of the early
centuries survived, automatically imposed certain restrictions.

In 1910 the Coptic Museum (*Chapter Five*) was founded in Old
Cairo, and in 1947 a new wing was added. The exhibits, which
represent the richest collection of Coptic art in the world,
have been exhibited according to media: stonework,
woodwork, metalwork, ivory carvings, tapestries, pottery,
glassware, and manuscripts. It is extremely difficult to
visualize them in context when one visits the museum. For
example, patriarchal chairs in woodwork in the old wing are
separated from the patriarchal crowns and ecclesiastical
vestments in the new wing. Wooden doors of ancient churches
and monasteries are on display far from their metal bolts and
keys. Similar themes in different media, like the portrayal of
the Virgin and Child or the use of the vine as a decorative
motif in stone carvings, wooden panels, and tapestries, cannot
be compared. And wide variations in style that developed in

different localities cannot be observed. Compounding the problem is the fact that the objects span fifteen hundred years, from the fourth to the nineteenth centuries!

Nor do the monastic centers of Egypt facilitate an understanding of artistic development, because of the continuous stages of construction and renovation of the churches, and because there were constant migrations of monks. Syrian monks came to Egypt in the eighth century, for example, ánd one of the monasteries of Wadi al Natrun was purchased by a Syrian who carried out considerable restoration. There were serious Bedouin raids from the seventh to the eighth centuries and a great deal of damage was done to the ancient buildings, which were restored in Fatimid times in the eleventh and twelfth centuries. The Fatimids themselves used local craftsmen, who were mostly Copts, for enlarging and embellishing the city of Cairo; when Copts executed designs and motifs that were acceptable to their Arab patrons, they did this as competently as they had, in classical times, produced classical themes for Greek patrons. In each case they adopted some of the motifs or designs for their own use. Therefore, when one visits the monasteries of Wadi al Natrun, it must be borne in mind that some wall paintings were Alexandrine-, Byzantine-, or Syrian-inspired, while some of the non-figurative work produced there, such as metalwork, wooden sanctuary screens, cabinets, and furniture, were made by Copts inspired by Islam.

There are two art forms in which continuity of craftsmanship can be traced, namely Coptic textiles and illuminated manuscripts. While the motifs in the former and the calligraphy in the latter changed from age to age, the artistic execution of the work, as well as the techniques and the materials used, were of longstanding tradition.

Weaving in the early centuries of the Christian era, as in earlier times, employed mainly linen, although there is also some evidence of silk-weaving. The techniques—the so-called tapestry-weave and loom weaving—were inherited from the ancient Egyptians. The width of the loom used in Coptic tapestries (and later for the weaving of Islamic fabrics) is the same as that in the time of the pharaohs, and the special 'Egyptian knot' was used as well. In the fourth century wool was introduced and a variant was loop-weaving, in which the weft was not pulled tight. Silk became popular in the sixth century and by the eighth century full clerical tunics were woven in linen and silk. The weaving of some is so fine as to appear more like embroidery.

Coptic textiles, which developed into one of the finest of all Coptic arts, included wall hangings, blankets, and curtains, in addition to garment trimmings. The motifs show great diversity and include classical and Greek–Egyptian themes: lively cupids, dancing girls riding marine monsters, or birds and animals woven into foliage. Fish and grapes were popular Christian motifs, as well as biblical scenes such as the Virgin on a donkey holding the Child Jesus in front of her. After Constantinople became the capital of the empire, the weavers' repertoire was increased and enriched with Byzantine and Persian themes. All the textiles show a great sense of liveliness in the stylized figures, and there was an eager market throughout the Roman world in late antiquity, especially for trimmings for clerical robes; most in demand were tunics of undyed linen onto which decorative woven bands were worked. Ordinary people, too, had decorated togas in late antiquity. After the Arab conquest, Copts wove textiles for Muslim patrons and the Arabic kufic script was introduced into their own designs, especially after Arabic replaced the Coptic language.

Coptic manuscripts fall into five main groups: those in Greek, those in Greek and Coptic, those in Coptic, those in Coptic and Arabic, and finally those in Arabic. (Copts started to translate their religious literature into Arabic in the twelfth century, and decorated the opening page with lavish pictures and with border designs.) There are also Aramaic texts, especially at the monastery of the Syrians at Wadi al Natrun. The art of illustrating texts dates to pharaonic times when prayers and liturgies were written on papyrus paper with reed pens and deposited in the tomb of the deceased. The mortuary texts were traced in black outline with catchwords written in red. They were illustrated with figures of Egyptian deities and protective symbols. These vignettes were frequently painted in bright colors with border designs at the top and bottom.

In the Christian era, religious writings were also written on papyrus paper and parchment, but the use of the codex was an innovation. Instead of sheets of papyrus pasted together to form strips and rolled, the pages were bound together into books. The pages were written in black, with red used for the titles and the beginnings of the chapters. Many were decorated with designs in bright colors including figures of martyrs, saints, apostles, and angels, as well as birds, animals, foliage, and geometrical designs. When, in the ninth century, a new writing material, paper—made from old linen rags—was introduced from the East, it derived its name from its Egyptian predecessor, papyrus, which continued to be used. Omar Tussun wrote in the late nineteenth century of a group of copyists at the monastery of Saint Macarius in Wadi al Natrun who were capable of drawing Coptic letters in the form of birds and figures. Calligraphy (now in Arabic only) is still an art form in Egypt, and Arabic calligraphers still use the reed pen.

It is fitting to conclude this chapter with Coptic painting, which is true art as against what we today call crafts. Coptic paintings reveal both an unsophisticated, almost crude style and a refined, highly developed one. The former may have emerged in the early years of Christianity when ancient temples were converted into churches. Pharaonic reliefs were covered with layers of plaster and Christian themes were painted on the stucco base. Wall paintings survive *in situ* in some places in Egypt including Bagawat in Kharga oasis, Saint Simeon's Monastery at Aswan, the White Monastery at Sohag, the monastery of Saint Macarius in Wadi al Natrun, and the sanctuary of the Ethiopian saint Takla Hamanout in the Hanging Church (al Muallaqa) in Old Cairo. Early wall paintings that have been transferred to the Coptic Museum include niches from the monasteries of Bawit and Sakkara, the former among the finest examples of their type. The Copts loved bright, clear color and were extremely talented in mixing different dyes and powdered rock, often using the white of an egg to combine them.

Icons, or images of sacred personalities painted on wooden panels, that are themselves regarded as sacred, were a later development. When it was realized that the war on paganism

Christ enthroned. Detail of painted niche from monastery of Bawit; now in Coptic Museum. Photograph by Robert Scott.

launched by the emperor Theodosius had not stopped pious people from sanctifying holy relics, the church authorized the painting of religious themes that would aid the faithful in an understanding of Christianity, especially scenes depicting the Nativity, the Virgin and Child, the apostles, and the lives of the saints. According to the Arab historian al Maqrizi, the patriarch Kirollos I hung icons in all the churches of Alexandria in the year 420 and then decreed that they should be hung in the other churches of Egypt as well.

In the earliest development of icon painting the artists worked directly on the wooden panel, but later they began to cover the surface with a soft layer of gypsum, onto which lines could be chiseled to control the flow of liquid gold. There is indication that more than one artist was involved in the production of a single work, but the face was painted by the master. Such division of labor resulted in greater production, but it also brought an end to any personal expression of piety such as had characterized the wall paintings. When Egypt turned increasingly towards Syria and Palestine after the schism in the fifth century, her saints and martyrs began to take on the stiff, majestic look characteristic of Syrian art. There began to appear an expression of spirituality rather than naivety on the faces of the subjects, more elegance in the drawing of the figures, and more use of gold backgrounds and richly adorned clerical garments.

Painters were not, at first, constrained by a rigid code. They were free to experiment with their themes. Consequently, there is a variety of interpretations in the treatment of a single subject that is quite striking. By the fifth and sixth centuries the angel Michael, for example, was painted sometimes with a sword, another time with a cross, and, on occasion, with a trumpet; he either wore a flowing robe or was clad in richly embroidered vestments. Such variations are especially notable in scenes of the Annunciation and the Nativity, which are seldom rendered twice with the same details.

Paintings produced in Egypt under Byzantine rule did not resemble the opulent frescoes and mosaics of the eastern Roman Empire, where art was state-sponsored between 550 and the conquest of the Turks in the fifteenth century. Saint

Catherine's Monastery in Sinai, however, a stronghold of the Melkite faction, and still today a Greek Orthodox outpost, was rebuilt in the golden age of Justinian and adorned with some of the finest Byzantine icons to be found in the world. Some were painted on site, others were imported from the provinces of the empire and from Constantinople itself.

After the Arab conquest of Egypt in the seventh century, paintings became progressively less 'Coptic' in character. This became even more apparent in the thirteenth century when the art of copying panels and miniatures started and Anba Gabriel produced exquisite and brilliantly adorned work. He set a standard for copyists. Little original work was now produced. By the seventeenth and eighteenth centuries, as already mentioned, painters like Ibrahim al Nassikh al Baghdady and Yuhanna the Armenian—who were among the greatest painters of icons in Egypt—turned to Syrian and Byzantine models for inspiration. Finally, Astasy al Rumi, the Greek artist, was commissioned by the Copts to paint many of the icons that today hang in the churches of Old Cairo.

OLD CAIRO

1) Coptic Museum (new wing)
2) Coptic Museum (old wing)
3) Hanging Church
4) Church of St. Sergius
5) Church of St. Barbara
6) Ben Ezra Synagogue
7) Greek Orthodox Church & Monastery
8) Tower of Roman Fortress of Babylon
9) Convent of St. George

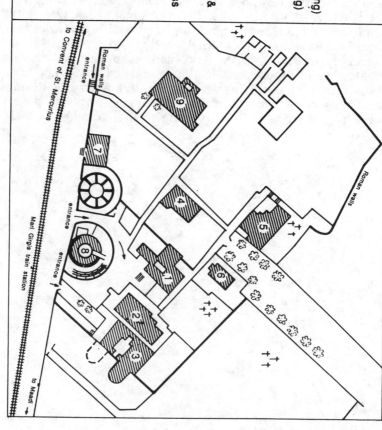

4

OLD CAIRO

Old Cairo, Masr al Qadima, lies within the old Roman fortress of Babylon, which was not only a walled but a heavily fortified city, with narrow streets and cobbled alleys. How the name of the famous Babylon of the Euphrates came to be echoed in Egypt is not known. The Coptic historian John of Nikiou, who lived at the time of the Arab invasion, claimed that it was originally built during the Persian occupation of Egypt (525–332 B.C.) and that it was at that time called the Fortress of Babylon. However, a much earlier visitor to the land of the Nile, the classical writer Diodorus Siculus, asserted that the name was brought by prisoners of war from great Babylon; the twelfth-dynasty pharaoh Senusert III, some two thousand years B.C., brought them to build public works. These Babylonians, Diodorus claimed, revolted against the Egyptians and built a fortification for protection, which had long fallen to ruin when the Persians came and repaired it.

When the Roman geographer Strabo came to Egypt in 24 B.C., he found that Old Cairo was, indeed, a fortress town and was occupied by three Roman garrisons. The emperor Trajan (98–117), it was said, cleared a canal that was running through the city, and included some urban areas into the enlarged fortress. By this time the area was known as the Castle of Babylon. Under the Christian emperor Arcadius (395–408), the Copts began to build numerous churches in and around Old Cairo. Forty-two are believed to have once stood in an area which extended northwards as far as today's Azbakiya Gardens, near Opera Square.

At the time of the Arab conquest in 641, Babylon was such a
sizable community that part of the fortress, including the huge
towers and bastions, was connected by walls to the newly
founded Arab capital of Fustat. The towers and bastions were
at first used as dwellings for the garrison. Later Amr ibn al As,
leader of the Arabs at the time of the conquest, returned to the
Copts land that the imperial government had taken from
them. When Fustat took over the role of capital from
Alexandria, the whole of Old Cairo was inhabited
exclusively by Copts, and the Arabs recruited local labor from
their ranks.

Early Coptic Churches

Coptic churches were rebuilt and restored time and again over
the centuries, often reusing wood and stonework. For this
reason some materials in a church may be of earlier date than
the structure itself. Although these early churches differ in
size and architectural features, they bear the unmistakable
stamp of a Coptic church. The axis of the building runs east to
west, with the entrance in the west and the high altar placed
in the east nearest the rising sun. The exteriors are
characterized by great simplicity and the churches are often
indistinguishable from neighboring, unadorned, brick
dwellings flanking a cobbled street; entry is often attained by
small side doors. The reason for this is that during attacks on
the Copts, churches were the first to suffer, and consequently
all exterior indication of their function was covered up.

The early churches have a simple ground plan in four main
divisions: the forecourt or narthex; the main body of the
church consisting of nave and side aisles; a narrow porch or
transept extending across the full width of the church; and the
inner chambers or sanctuary. The nave, which has an arched
timber roof higher than that of the side aisles, is separated
from the aisles (also arched with timber) by columns with
arches supporting a second row of columns superimposed on
them, which provide light from the clerestory. Figures of
saints were painted on the shafts of the columns, which were
frequently taken from earlier Greek or Roman buildings.

There was a low parapet with curtains separating the main
body of the church from the sanctuary, which was usually

Street decoration in Old Cairo. Photograph by Robert Scott.

erected on rising ground and ascended by a few steps. Later the parapet became a rail or screen beyond which only those in holy orders might pass. The sanctuary screen is made of wood, decorated with geometrical inlaid segments of ebony and ivory, often of intricate workmanship. Behind the screen are three domed apses, or *haikals*, which form separate chapels. The central apse holds the altar of the saint to whom the church is dedicated. The two side apses, dedicated to other saints, are used either on the feast days of those saints or whenever there is more than one celebration of the divine liturgy, as it is not permitted to take communion more than once per day at any one 'church' or altar.

Coptic altars are free-standing and are situated in the middle of the haikal. Above the altar is a wooden canopy resting on pillars. The side chapels are sometimes raised above the level of the transept but the central apse which holds the altar, with few exceptions, stands level with the transept. Behind the central altar there is a tribunal of semi-circular stone steps within the haikal, with a throne for a bishop and seats for the officiating clergy. A niche in the wall usually holds a sanctuary lamp, known as the perpetual lamp.

In the early years of Christianity, it was customary to bury the bodies of saints or martyrs beneath the altar, in a vault or crypt under the floor of the sanctuary. Today, most Coptic churches still possess relics, either enclosed in a casket covered by silk brocade, or kept beneath glass beside a picture of the patron saint. They are never on display. Some of the desert churches that date to the Middle Ages have reliquaries containing entire bodies, but it is more usual for the relics to be clothing of the saint, pieces of bone, hair, or even teeth. When the relics are in portable caskets, they can be removed and carried in procession for the healing of the sick or for important religious celebrations.

One of the earliest surviving churches in the world, the church of Saint Sergius (Abu Sarga) in the heart of Old Cairo, was planned in accordance with early church rituals. Candidates for baptism were first received in a small antechamber and then descended three steps into the baptistry, where they were immersed in water. When the rite was completed they received the eucharist and only then were

*Wood inlay altar screen and icons. Church of Saint Sergius,
Old Cairo. Photograph by Cassandra Vivian.*

allowed to enter the church. Purification before entering a holy place was of ancient origin. Only later was the baptistry moved to the side of the narthex of a church (but still outside the nave and aisles), and later still constructed at the end of the north aisle near the altar. Today, most churches have their baptistry near the sanctuary. The baptistry font is a basin deep enough to allow the priest to immerse a person totally in the water while pronouncing the baptismal formulary. In the narthex of some ancient churches there is an oblong tank or plunge bath, now covered by floorboards. It was used for baptism at Epiphany, for which service a portable basin is now used. Similarly, a shallow rectangular basin, also sunk in the floor, was used for the foot-washing service on Maundy Thursday and on the feast of Saints Peter and Paul.

The pulpits of Coptic churches have a distinctive straight-sided balcony on a raised platform. The polygonal pulpits found for example at Wadi al Natrun are rare in Coptic churches and are inevitably of modern date. The lectern usually stands before the door to the sanctuary. It is made of wood, sometimes inlaid with geometrical designs in ivory. The use of ostrich eggs in Coptic churches, where they are hung in front of the sanctuary screen, is of uncertain origin. Copts explain that they symbolize God's ever-vigilant eye. Another explanation may be rooted in tradition: the myth of the origin of life from an egg, especially the primordial egg, is recurrent in ancient Egyptian mythology. Ostrich eggs, and pottery eggs, are also used as decorative elements in mosques.

Church of Saint Sergius (Abu Sarga)

The church of Saint Sergius is situated to the north of the Coptic Museum, down a narrow cobbled lane, and lies some three meters below street level. The church is dedicated to two Roman officers, Sergius and Bacchus, who were martyred in Syria in 303. The earliest part of the building dates from the fifth century and was built over the cave where, according to tradition, the Holy Family hid during their Flight into Egypt. The structure was burnt down and restored in the eighth century. The whole of the church was again restored and partially rebuilt during the Fatimid era (tenth to twelfth centuries). Despite restoration and reconstruction, the church

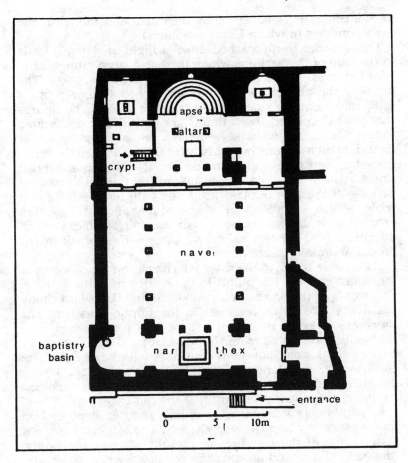

The church of Saint Sergius

of Saint Sergius is nevertheless regarded as a model of the early churches in which Copts worshiped.

The entrance is approached down a flight of stairs. It leads to the side of the narthex, where there is a large plunge-bath, boarded over. At the end of the narthex is the baptistry. The nave of the church, which has an arched timber roof, is separated from the side aisles by marble pillars. The figures that once decorated the columns are only dimly discernible today. On the right-hand wall is a Biblia Pauperum that includes such commemorative occasions as Christ's birth, miracles, baptism, and resurrection; it dates to medieval times. Also in the church is an interesting thirteenth-century carving of the Last Supper. Jesus sits with his disciples at a table, which is of similar shape to an ancient Egyptian offering table. Indeed, a Coptic altar closely resembles such an offering table. It has a raised molding with a break in the border to drain off water.

The marble pulpit in the nave, which rests on ten columns, is a modern copy of the pulpit in the church of Saint Barbara. Fragments of the original rosewood pulpit, inlaid with ebony and ivory, are now preserved in the Coptic Museum. The sanctuary screen is decorated with several panels which may originally have come from the leaves of a door. The upper part contains small panels of ebony set with large crosses of solid ivory, exquisitely chiseled with scrollwork. Lower down, the ivory is set in arabesque shapes. The icons are of the twelve apostles, with the Virgin at the center.

Brass oil lamps hang from the ceiling, and two steps lead up to the sanctuary and the side chapels. The original canopied altar is one of the treasures of the old wing of the Coptic Museum. The central apse wall is encrusted with marble and decorated with mosaics. Parts of the original paintings can still be seen in the dome. The side chapels contain numerous icons including one of the Flight into Egypt, where Mary (shown on a mule) is wearing a crown and holding Jesus, followed by Joseph and Mary Magdalene.

The crypt, where the Holy Family are believed to have hidden during the Flight into Egypt, lies to the left of the sanctuary. The original cave was situated beneath the center of the transept. It was turned into a three-aisled chapel, with an altar in the wall in the form of a tomb-recess. A commemorative mass is celebrated in the church of Saint Sergius on June l, which the Copts believe to be the day of the Flight. [Despite current restoration of this famous church, which is scheduled for completion by the end of 1990, visitors are allowed to see the crypt.]

Hanging Church (al Muallaqa)

This church dedicated to the Virgin Mary is known as the 'Hanging' or 'Suspended' Church because it rests on the two southwestern bastions of the old Roman fortress of Babylon. Its nave extends over the portal that led into the ancient fortress. Some parts of the original church still survive, notably the section that lies to the right of the sanctuary, on top of the southern bastion of the fortress.

The Hanging Church was the seat of the bishop of Babylon (i.e. Fustat) in the seventh century. In the ninth century the church was destroyed, but when it was restored in the eleventh century, it was made the seat of the Coptic patriarchate. At this time it became the center to which theologians, lawyers, and astronomers came for study. The church underwent periodic renovation from medieval right through to modern times. Some of the wood and stonework were reused, so that they date to an earlier period than the structure in which they are housed. Also, some parts of this church, and of others in Old Cairo, have been taken to the Coptic Museum: for example a sycamore panel from over the doorway of the Hanging Church and the pinewood altar-dome from the church of Saint Sergius.

The entrance gateway to the Hanging Church leads to a stairway, which gives onto a passage and a covered courtyard. The outer porch, decorated with glazed tiles in geometrical designs, dates to the eleventh century.

The main part of the church has a wide central nave and narrow side aisles, marked off by eight columns on each side. The vaulted timber roof has recently been restored. The columns have Corinthian capitals, indicating they were usurped from earlier buildings. With one exception in black basalt, they are of white marble. They were once painted with figures of saints, but only a single column still bears the traces of a figure, badly faded. There are three other columns in the center of the nave, in the right half of which is the pulpit. The pulpit, with its straight-sided balcony, is thought to be among the earliest surviving. It is assigned to the eleventh century but some of the material of which it is made may be earlier. It is of marble, and rests on fifteen delicate columns arranged in seven pairs with a leader, symbolizing the seven sacraments of the church. The columns of each pair are identical, but no two pairs are alike.

The inlaid woodwork of this church is among the finest to be found. Cedarwood and ivory were used for the sanctuary screen. The ivory is carved into segments of exquisite design and set in the woodwork to form the Coptic cross, which has arms of even length, each with three end points symbolizing the Blessed Trinity. At the top of the sanctuary screen is a series of icons representing Christ enthroned (center); the Virgin, the archangel Gabriel, and Saint Peter (right); and Saint John the Baptist, the archangel Michael, and Saint Paul (left).

Behind the sanctuary screen is the altar. High altars in Coptic churches are covered by a canopy resting on four columns. The side altars are sometimes similarly covered. The central altar of the Hanging Church is dedicated to the Blessed Virgin and the side altars to Saint John the Baptist on the right and Saint George on the left. Saint George, a Roman legionary, defied Diocletian and suffered martyrdom in Asia. His body is said to have been brought to Egypt by the Coptic patriarch Gabriel II in the twelfth century.

A small church dedicated to Takla Hamanout, the Ethiopian saint, leads off from the main church, to the right, near the transept. It is of uncertain date, although the screen that separates it from the main church dates to the thirteenth century, and is worthy of note. It is regarded as one of the finest pieces of craftsmanship, and one of the highest examples of Coptic woodwork, of the thirteenth century. It is made of wood and mother-of-pearl, and when illuminated from behind with a candle (available close by for this purpose) the segments glow with a rose tint.

Two wall paintings in the chapel of the much venerated Ethiopian saint are noteworthy even though badly faded. One

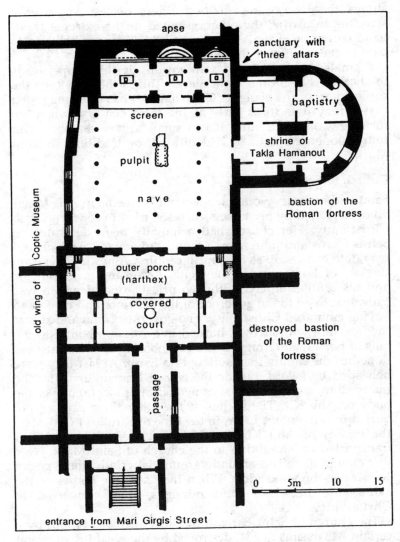

apse

sanctuary with three altars

baptistry

screen

shrine of Takla Hamanout

pulpit

bastion of the Roman fortress

n a v e

Coptic Museum

outer porch (narthex)

covered court

destroyed bastion of the Roman fortress

old wing of

passage

0 5m 10 15

entrance from Mari Girgis Street

The Hanging Church

shows the twenty-four haloed elders of the Apocalypse standing in a row; the other, situated in the extreme right-hand corner, is of the Virgin and Child. They are believed to date to the twelfth or thirteenth century.

A small, newly restored stairway inside this chapel leads to another chapel on a higher level. This is thought to be the earliest part of the Hanging Church and it has been suggested that it may date to as early as the third century, when the fortress walls were built. It is a small square chamber with four wooden columns. It is dedicated, by tradition, to Saint Mark.

Church of Saint Barbara

Saint Barbara was a young woman of Nicomedia in Asia Minor who was killed by her father when she tried to convert him to Christianity. Her church had originally been dedicated to Saints Cyrus and John (Abu Kir and Yuhanna in Arabic), and may date to as early as the fourth century. Abu Kir came from the city of Damanhur in the Delta. According to legend, he and his brother agreed with two priests, one of whom was Yuhanna, to go to the governor of the province and confess to having embraced Christianity. The governor commanded that they be shot with arrows, burned in a furnace, bound to the tails of horses, and dragged to a neighboring city. All this was done but the saintly men suffered no harm. At last they were beheaded by sword outside the city of Damanhur. After the martyrdom, some holy men came and built a church over the body of Abu Kir. The bodies of the other three saints were buried in Damanhur. Later, in the time of Kirollos I (408–450), the bodies of Abu Kir and Yuhanna were exhumed and transported to Alexandria to the church of Saint Mark. Near that church there was an underground labyrinth where pagan worshipers honored idols. When they saw the bodies of the saints and heard of their miracles, they converted to Christianity.

The church of Saint Barbara in Old Cairo was rebuilt by a certain Athanasius in 684, destroyed by the great fire of Fustat in 750, and subsequently restored in the eleventh century. Later, when the relics of Saint Barbara were transported there, a new sanctuary was added to house them.

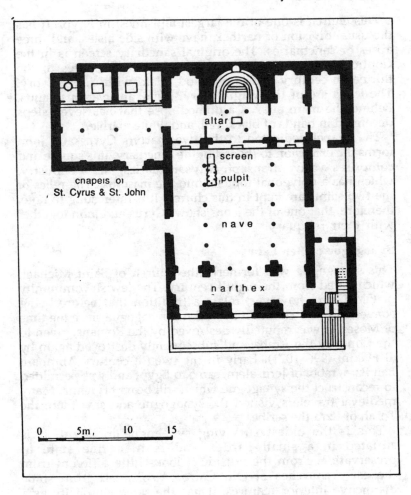

altar

screen

pulpit

cnapeis or
St. Cyrus & St. John

nave

narthex

0   5m,   10   15

The church of Saint Barbara

This church is one of the largest and finest in Egypt. It has the usual division of narthex, nave with side aisles, and three apses or sanctuaries. The original sanctuary screen is in the Coptic Museum. The one now in the church dates to the thirteenth century and is of wood inlaid with carved ivory. The icons are of the Virgin Mary, Jesus, and various saints. Behind the main altar is a domed apse that has seven steps decorated in bands of black, red, and white marble.

The chapel dedicated to the two martyrs Cyrus and John forms the extension to the left of the sanctuary. It is square and comprises a nave, transept, two sanctuaries, and a baptistry, which has a polygonal font set into the masonry. The relics of the two saints are kept in this church. It is interesting to note, therefore, that one of the icons shows Cyrus and John together with their reliquary.

Synagogue of Ben Ezra

This synagogue was formerly the church of Saint Michael, which dated from the eighth century. The Jewish community of Old Cairo, however, relate a tradition that before being converted into a church it had been a synagogue since the time of Moses. It was reputedly destroyed by the Romans, given to the Copts by the Arabs, and subsequently destroyed again by al Hakim (996–1021). Early in the twelfth century Abraham Ben Ezra, rabbi of Jerusalem, came to Egypt and was permitted to reconstruct the synagogue which still bears his name. Many medieval travelers visited the synagogue and saw there the Torah of Ezra the scribe.

This is the oldest surviving synagogue in Egypt. It is situated in a small garden and is in a fine state of preservation. From the outside it looks little different from the early churches of Old Cairo. Also, apart from some distinctive interior features, it has the same simplicity as a Coptic church. Most of the decorative work, especially in wood and mother-of-pearl, dates to the twelfth century. Renovation of the synagogue was started some years ago and is scheduled for completion by the end of 1990.

The Star of David adorns the central marble bimah (pulpit), which is double-sided. The bimah was used for the reading of the scriptures, which were later rolled up and put away in cupboards in a wooden screen. Above the cupboards are the Ten Commandments, and in front is the seven-branched candelabrum, the menorah.

At the end of the nineteenth century, when clearance of accumulated rubbish was being made to the rear of the synagogue, a great part of the Hebrew Book of Ecclesiastes was found, as well as numerous secular writings. These latter were rare original documents that date to the eleventh and twelfth centuries. Known collectively as the Geniza Documents, the unique discovery includes such miscellaneous items as marriage contracts, trading activities, even outstanding bills, and is regarded as one of the most remarkable literary finds in modern times, as it casts a floodlight on various aspects of Jewish life in medieval Cairo.

Convent of Saint George

This convent, which was described in glowing terms by al Maqrizi in the fifteenth century, is today inhabited by about thirty nuns. A small door from the narrow, cobbled streets of Old Cairo leads into the peaceful courtyard. A stairway leads down to the most ancient part of the convent, where there is a remarkable hall dating to the tenth century. This has a high ceiling and doors around it that give onto fourteen small cells. The shrine containing the icon of Saint George is approached through a wooden doorway, the leaves of which are over six meters high. The custodians of the shrine are proud to display a chain, of uncertain origin, that they claim was used to tie up martyrs.

Convent and Church of Saint Mercurius (Abu Seifein)

The convent of Saint Mercurius (with resident nuns) lies outside the walls of the old Roman fortress, but within easy distance of it. This monastic site is the first in Egypt to be named after the martyr Mercurius, and is one of the largest and oldest in greater Cairo. It was built in the sixth century and has been destroyed and rebuilt on no less than four occasions, the most important reconstruction taking place in the tenth century. At one time it was used for storage of sugar-cane.

Mercurius, Abu Seifein ('He of Two Swords'), was a Roman legionary who defied the emperor Decius. One night he had a vision in which an angel gave him a second, luminous sword to fight against paganism. He became a Christian and after a long struggle and terrible persecutions he suffered martyrdom. He was buried in Palestine but his remains were transferred to Old Cairo in the fifteenth century. Some of his relics lie beneath the main icon of the saint near the altar of the church that bears his name; others are in the neighboring convent.

Recent reconstruction of this huge monastic site has been a challenge. It contains so many treasures that it is known as the School of Coptic Art. Among its most valuable objects are exquisitely carved marble windows and superlative wood and ivory work, in addition to an extraordinary collection of icons of saints, martyrs, patriarchs, bishops, and monks, and a series relating to the Old and the New Testaments.

The church of Saint Mercurius comprises a main church and four large chapels annexed to it on the first and second floors. The chapel on the ground floor is dedicated to Saint Jacob. The three chapels on the upper floor are dedicated to the 144,000 children killed by Herod; to Saint George; and to John the Baptist.

A special feature of the main church is the large plunge-bath in the narthex, which is not covered by boards. Likewise, the shallow basin in the main body of the church can be seen. Careful cleaning of some of the marble columns within the church has revealed paintings on their shafts. The two columns that flank the sanctuary screen, for example, show Christ holding the gospel in His left hand and with His right hand raised in blessing; and a painting of the Virgin and Child. Most such early work on usurped marble columns has disappeared, and these are rare survivals.

Above the main altar of the church is a fine wooden altar-canopy in the form of a dome resting on woodwork with open-pointed arches. Each of the eight faces at the corners of the arches has scenes from the Old and New Testaments relating to the altar, which dates back to the beginning of the tenth century. Dominating the wall of the main haikal is a recently restored painting of Jesus and the twelve apostles in the resurrection scene, symbolically crowned by an eagle, representing Jesus, standing astride the serpent that represents death.

The two side apses of the church are dedicated to the angel Raphael and the Holy Virgin. There is a baptistry in the apse of the chapel of the angel Raphael with a shallow font. A second font for the baptism of adults is located outside the main church, in the chapel of Saint Jacob.

The convent of Saint Mercurius is famous for its association with a holy man, Saint Barsum, or Barsum the Naked, who died in 1317 having spent twenty years of his life in strict isolation in the tiny dark crypt with its low vaulted roof. This can be entered by a flight of stairs near the north aisle of the church.

Beneath the stucco in the chapel of Saint George, on the upper floor, layers of unique wall paintings from different periods of early Christianity were found during restoration.

Church of Saint Shenuda

The church of Saint Shenuda, situated some twenty meters beyond the church of Saint Mercurius, was originally built in the seventh century in honor of the famous Coptic saint whose name it bears. The main body of the church comprises three aisles separated by two rows of ten marble columns each. The sanctuary screen, of red cedarwood inlaid with wheel and cross patterns in ivory, bears a row of seven icons; at the center is the Virgin, the remaining six each showing a pair of apostles.

The church of Saint Shenuda typifies, in many ways, the change and continuity to be found in Egypt. One of the most ancient churches in Old Cairo, the building was originally constructed on the earliest plan for church rituals, with the baptistry and a shallow foot-washing basin (both now covered up) in the antechamber of the church. In the time of al Hakim, early in the eleventh century, the church was used as a mosque and the call to prayer was made from it. It was reconstructed and renovated in the fourteenth century, and renovated several times in the nineteenth century. The most recent restoration was completed in the last few years.

Monastery of Saint Menas

The monastery of Saint Menas, Babilun al Darag, situated in the northern part of Old Cairo, north of the Roman aqueduct, is the place where the relics of Saint Menas were kept in the main church until sent to Maryut in 1962.

* * *

One is most conscious of a sense of history in Old Cairo. A fascinating example of overlapping ideologies may be seen in the two towers of the old Roman fortress (between which is the gateway leading to the Coptic Museum.) Built on top of the northern tower is the Greek Orthodox church of Saint George (Mari Girgis). And immediately to the south of the southern tower is the Coptic Orthodox Hanging Church (al Muallaqa). Moreover, some of the material in the tower, which is of dressed stone with alternating courses of bricks, bears hieroglyphic inscriptions, attesting to the reuse of stone from ancient temples.

5

THE COPTIC MUSEUM

The Coptic Museum, which possesses the richest collection of Coptic art in the world, lies within the old Roman fortress of Babylon in Old Cairo. It was founded in 1910 by Marcus Simaika, a wealthy Copt who felt that a special building should be devoted to Coptic antiquities. He raised funds by public subscription and used his personal influence to acquire important artifacts from old Coptic houses. The museum was built on land belonging to the Coptic patriarchate. In 1931 the Egyptian Government gave it official recognition and sympathetic support. The new wing was built in 1947 and two years later the collection hitherto in the Cairo Museum was transferred there. In 1983–84 the museum was completely renovated as part of the restoration program set in motion by the Antiquities Organization.

The exhibits in the Coptic Museum are a bridge between the Cairo Museum of (pharaonic) Antiquities, the Greco–Roman Museum in Alexandria (which has some Coptic items), and the Islamic Museum in Cairo. The objects have been grouped according to medium: stonework, metalwork, tapestries, and manuscripts in the new wing; woodwork, pottery, and glassware in the old.

The museum is approached through an elegantly laid-out garden with gazebos and benches. There are some fine pieces of decorative stonework in the garden, including an open-work limestone window decoration with floral designs in relief surrounding an Asian elephant at the center. This and most of the other monuments in the garden are of uncertain date and provenance. A flight of stairs leads down to the entrance of the museum.

New Wing: Ground Floor

The ground floor of the new wing is devoted to stone objects and wall paintings from monasteries in Middle and Upper Egypt. The entrance hall forms chamber *A*, containing niches and carvings from Ihnasya, near Beni Suef in Middle Egypt. They were found in the rubble of a churchyard and were overlooked for many years. They date to the fourth and fifth centuries of the Christian era but the subject matter is nevertheless typical of a pagan Greek community. Each piece is carved with mythological characters and motifs: the nude figures of Aphrodite in a shell, Leda and the swan, Europa and the bull, Dionysos with bunches of grapes, and the goat-hoofed Pan seducing a dancer holding a sistrum, to mention a few. Although the subject matter is wholly classical, with no Christian symbolism whatsoever, they are typically Coptic in spirit. That is to say, the style is distinct from that of similar reliefs to be found in Alexandria, Rome, and Constantinople. The carvings from Ihnasya are more crudely done and have certain distinctive characteristics that point to their execution by Coptic artists, like the front-view faces with large, expressive eyes.

Chamber *B* contains more niches and stelae of the same period, but from a Christian burial ground. The use of classical and Egyptian symbolism is clear. For example, a pair of dolphins remains but in place of a sea-nymph at the center there is a cross. A man with a child in his arms has a cross in the form of an ancient Egyptian ankh, or key of life, above his head. On the left-hand wall of the chamber there is evidence of the development of the cross in Egypt; some of the early examples are identical with the ankh, while others are variants of it, and one shows the ankh with a cross inside the loop at the top. Egyptian influence is also clear on the limestone fragment of a burial scene at the center of the wall that shows the deceased lying on a bier with two figures, one at the head and one at the feet, much as the goddesses Isis and Nephthys are depicted at each end of ancient sarcophagi. The column at the center of the chamber combines Byzantine and

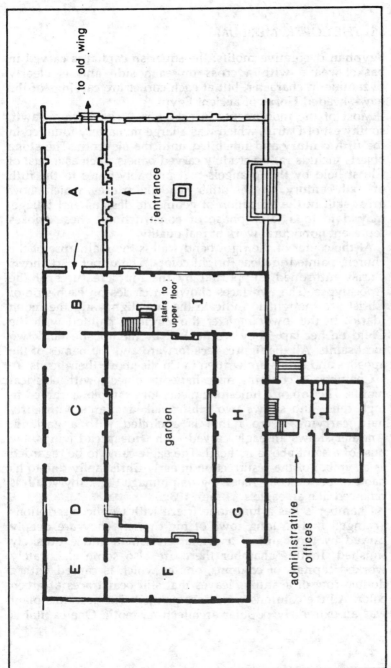

The Coptic Museum: new wing, ground floor

Egyptian decorative motifs: the squarish capital is carved in basket-weave with a cross on each side and is clearly Byzantine in character, but at each corner are carvings of the hawk-headed Horus of ancient Egypt.

Most of the monuments in chamber *C* come from Bawit, southwest of Dairut, which was a large monastery founded in the fifth century and inhabited until the eleventh. The stone objects include rather crudely carved panels, such as a bust of Christ held by flying angels that probably dates to the fifth or sixth century. On the other hand the friezes, which show great skill in the execution of geometric designs and foliage, may date to a later phase of construction. These friezes represent nonfigural work of real quality.

At the center of the right-hand wall is the main apse of the church, painted in clear, bright colors. The upper part shows Christ enthroned, supported by the four creatures of the Apocalypse. The two faces shown in circles on each side of Christ are thought to indicate the sun (light) and the moon (dark). In the lower register the Virgin is painted with the Child on her lap. They are flanked by the apostles and two local saints. All the figures face forward and the names of the apostles and saints are written in Coptic above their heads.

Chamber *D* contains miscellaneous objects with classical motifs. The top of a limestone niche, for example, is carved in high relief and shows two plump naked infants with curly hair, carrying a cross that is encircled with a garland. Another shows an eagle carved with widespread wings, the bust of a saint above its head. The eagle came to be regarded as a symbol of the resurrection in early Christianity due to its habit of periodically renewing its plumage (". . . thy youth is renewed like an eagle's." Psalm 103:5).

Chamber *E* has a limestone frieze with Coptic inscriptions arranged in two long rows of high relief. They are deeply carved by the hand of a master craftsman and exquisitely finished. In this chamber there are also some elaborately worked capitals of columns, one of which is carved with a double row of acanthus leaves that still bear traces of green color. All the columns were once painted. The acanthus plant was an extremely popular architectural motif. One capital is decorated with leaves and branches that appear to be swayed by the wind.

All the monuments in chamber *F* come from the monastery of Saint Jeremias at Sakkara, which was built in the fifth century. The site was first excavated between 1908 and 1910 by J.E. Quibell and recently re-excavated and studied by Dr. P. Grossman of the German Archaeological Institute in 1980–81. The columns are arranged in pairs the full length of the hall. Their deeply-carved capitals are decorated with acanthus leaves, palm-fronds, the lotus, and vine leaves—some have tendrils and bunches of grapes combined in interesting variations. Limestone particularly lends itself to deep carving, and the resulting contrast of light and shade, which was a stylistic development of Greek art, continued in late antiquity and later in Coptic art. No shafts of the columns were found on site. They were probably taken for reuse in later monuments. It is interesting to learn that the archaeologists excavating this monastery found that the monks themselves had reused stone from a neighboring pharaonic burial ground.

The painted niches on the right-hand wall are in an excellent state of preservation. One shows the seated Virgin with the Child on her lap and with Christ painted above them in the dome. The niche in the rear right-hand corner of the chamber shows Mary seated with the child Jesus at her breast. Representation of the suckling of infants has its origin in ancient Egypt: in the temple of Khonsu at Karnak the god Horus is shown at the breast of the goddess Mut, and many scenes on ostraca from Deir al Madina feature the suckling of infants. Bronze statuettes of the goddess Isis seated with Horus on her lap have also been found in their hundreds throughout Egypt and, indeed, the Hellenistic world.

The sixth-century stone pulpit at the center of the rear wall, with a stairway leading up to a cubical, is noteworthy. It resembles the stairs and shrines in the Heb–Sed court of the funerary complex of the pharaoh Zoser, which is situated some five hundred meters away from the monastery on the Sakkara plateau. The proximity of the two structures points to a possible link between their architectural features. However, the pulpit, which has Coptic texts inscribed on the two sides, has a decorative motif in the shape of a shell at the top, which is a Hellenistic symbol.

Chamber *G* contains miscellaneous stone sculpture that is reminiscent of the Greek–Egyptian heritage. For example, turning to the right there is a small carving of a sphinx between the columns of a Greek temple, on the right-hand wall a frieze of the grape harvest. The latter is somewhat crudely executed but recalls scenes of rural activity depicted in the tombs of ancient Egyptian noblemen on the necropolis. It shows, from the left, musicians in the field, followed by various stages of collecting and transporting the harvest, ending with a camel (not a donkey as in the ancient tombs—the earliest evidence of camels in Egypt is towards the end of the first century). The persistence of tradition in the early years of Christianity is exemplified in this frieze. It must be remembered that because the people of the Nile Valley were largely illiterate, a symbolic scene such as the grape harvest was something they could appreciate because it was an activity that defied political or religious change.

Biblical themes from the Old and New Testaments dominate in chamber *H*. Left of the entrance doorway is a niche showing Abraham and Isaac with the sacrificial lamb, a carving of the enthroned Christ with two angels, and another of three men in a fiery furnace with a fourth man who is probably a savior. Such themes were common throughout the Roman world but these carvings have a folk simplicity that is typical of Coptic sculpture. All the figures face forwards and have heads that are somewhat large in relation to the bodies. These characteristics are difficult to explain, apart from the obvious inclination of the early Egyptian Christians to move away from the canons and style of Hellenistic art towards a more personal expression of their faith. The objects on the opposite wall include a relief of the Virgin and Child showing Mary raising an arm from the elbow in a gesture of piety. Another has a central figure that is difficult to identify (it could be Christ), flanked by angels or magi; the feet appear to float above the ground and the figures have halos around their heads.

The reliefs to the rear of this chamber combine the human figure with plant and animal motifs. That is to say, the figures form part of the decorative design, especially friezes of hunters and animals in thickets. Though crude in execution they are nevertheless forceful and expressive.

On the right-hand wall of chamber *I* is a large polychrome wall painting. It shows four figures, representing Adam and Eve in the Garden of Eden, before and after their fall. The two figures to the right show the pair innocent and unashamed. Then, to the left, after having taken of the forbidden fruit, they are covering themselves. The serpent is painted next to Eve, and Adam raises his fingers in accusation. This mural comes from the village of Omm al Beregat in the Fayoum and dates to the eleventh century. Also in this chamber are nonfigural paintings with decorative geometrical designs in muted colors.

Moving towards the stairway leading to the upper floor, we come to a large squarish-shaped capital carved in typical Byzantine basketweave and decorated with the ancient Egyptian lotus and papyrus plants, representing Upper and Lower Egypt, bound together in the symbol of unity.

New Wing: Upper Floor

Moving clockwise around the first chamber (*J*) we come to a painted wooden mummy case, which is excellently preserved. It is decorated with a full-length portrait of the deceased who wears a robe to the ankles. Around the head is a floral garland, like the ancient Egyptian 'wreath of justification,' which became associated by early Christians with the wreath of thorns. Whether the mummy case was from a pagan or a Christian burial ground is not clear.

There are several large tapestries in this chamber. They are parts of curtains. One hanging features a dark-skinned, dancing flute player. Beside him is a vertical panel decorated with pairs of warriors and dancing girls and, in the center, a rectangle containing three circles, each with a figure of a man on horseback. The other tapestries are woven with dancers, warriors, and musical ceremonies. One is a heavy piece, woven of wool and linen, with geometric designs at the edges and peacocks and an animal like a calf at the center. All the tapestries in this chamber show Hellenistic and Byzantine influence.

Coptic textile, Coptic Museum.
Photograph courtesy of Coptic Museum.

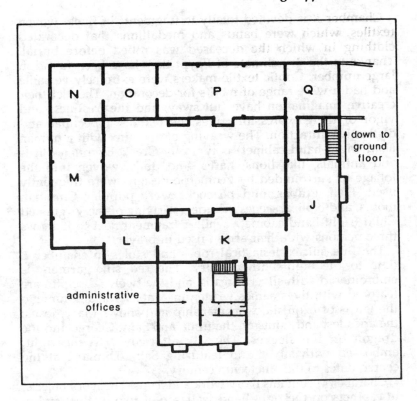

The Coptic Museum: new wing, upper floor

Chamber K is devoted totally to fragments of finely woven textiles, which were bands and medallions that decorated clothing in which the deceased was robed before burial. Thanks to the dry climate of Egypt they have been found in large number. Coptic textile makers were extremely versatile and had a wide range of motifs for decoration. They let their creative imagination have full sway, and the freshness and vigor of their expression gives the textiles a peculiar and distinctive attraction. The weaving of a sphinx with a human head (right-hand cabinet) is typically Greek–Egyptian. Birds and animals, like lions, hares, and dogs, woven into the foliage or surrounded by geometric designs were frequently used. Fish, grapes, and peacocks were popular Christian motifs, and biblical scenes include a weaving of the Virgin and Child (right-hand cabinet), while a fragment next to it shows three persons with their arms raised in prayer.

The fine silk ecclesiastical robes and stoles in chamber L date to the eighteenth century. The red silk garment is embroidered with silver threads, and the twelve disciples are featured with their names written in Arabic. The silk tunic to the left is of exquisite workmanship and shows Mary, Jesus, the apostles, and saints on the front, and Saint George and the dragon on the sleeves. The silk altar-cover to the right, embossed with silver and featuring Saint Dimiana at the center, dates to the nineteenth century.

Chamber M contains ivory work and icons. The ivory objects, in cabinets on the right-hand wall, are of two distinct styles: the classical elegance of the Alexandrine style, showing a taste for elaborate ornamentation; and rather unrefined ivories that were found in Upper Egypt. The former objects include seals, bracelets, and small boxes, as well as combs. One of the most noteworthy is a comb carved on the one side with a scene of the raising of Lazarus and the healing of the blind man, and on the other side with two angels holding a garland framing a saint riding a horse. Some of the ivory work shows festive scenes; in particular, one of the boxes shows well-dressed, elegant ladies in lavish robes. Although Christian principles regarded luxury and a display of vanity as a fault, women of means did not give up their coquetry. A great many exquisite toilet objects have been found among the Coptic antiquities. The panels with Coptic inscriptions should be noted. They are examples of perfect carving and finish, clearly indicating pride in workmanship. There are also objects that are crude in execution, such as the figurines that may have been made by the monks themselves. They were found in one of the churches of Old Cairo.

The icons in this chamber are mostly of late date, from the seventeenth and eighteenth centuries. Many of them show the saints in stiff postures, bereft of the freshness of early Coptic art, and they include scenes of suffering, which is not a local characteristic. The artist's name and the date are often inscribed, in Coptic and Arabic, at the bottom of the picture.

An icon with a complex theme that is typically Byzantine in character shows the resurrection of Jesus, who is portrayed as a soldier; around the empty sepulcher are Roman soldiers, two of them sleeping. Another noteworthy icon depicts Saint Menas on horseback, holding a bridle and fixing a dragon with a spear bearing a cross at the top; this icon is a good example of simple panel painting executed in muted colors. An icon of two dog-headed saints bears witness to the persistence of ancient tradition.

The saints most frequently depicted on icons are Saint George, Saint Michael the Archangel, Saint Barbara, Saint Mark the Evangelist, Saint Antony and Saint Paul. To the left of the doorway leading into the next chamber is an icon showing Saint Antony and Saint Paul, the two great ascetics whose monasteries are near the Red Sea (see p.127). The direct, front-view faces and large expressive eyes are typical of Coptic art but the execution of the work shows Syrian influence. According to Coptic tradition, the food of Saint Paul was half a loaf of bread brought miraculously every day by a crow, but on the occasion of the visit of Saint Antony, the crow (painted between the two figures) brought a whole loaf.

Several rooms are devoted to a remarkable collection of objects of various periods in silver, bronze, copper, and iron. They include both religious and secular items. Among the objects of a religious nature are eucharistic vessels and altar furniture, like chalices, spoons, and patens, as well as chandeliers, sanctuary lamps, and pilgrimage flasks. The secular items include jewelry and a whole range of kitchen utensils, such as weights, measures, and ladles.

In chamber N some elaborately adorned patriarchal staffs dating to the twelfth century are worth noting. Such a staff, which the Copts call the 'staff of authority,' is used only for ornamental purposes. The plain silver-headed staff or mace, known as the pastoral staff, is the one carried by the Coptic patriarch and all his bishops on ceremonial occasions.

There is also an excellent collection of crosses. In the middle cabinet on the rear wall is one shaped like the ancient Egyptian ankh, with a Christian cross in the loop at the top. It is interesting to note that the crucifix is not used on altars of the Coptic church. A hand-cross, however, is used for ceremonial purposes when the priest blesses the congregation, after which it is always placed flat. Moreover, the fan, or flabellum, which is also displayed here, was used in the earliest church services, although its function is not known with certainty. The elaborate metal book caskets attest to refined production of metalwork in the tenth and eleventh centuries. They were used for protecting the Holy Writ. Later, when copies of the Bible multiplied, it is possible that the delicate, aged originals were sealed in the caskets and regarded as valuable relics.

In the center of chamber O is a fine statue of a Roman eagle that was found in the fortress of Babylon. This strongest of all birds of prey, reputed for its keen sight and unmatched ability in flight, was adopted by the Roman Empire as a symbol of splendor and grandeur. To the right there are two helmets, one with four gilded crosses. Between them is a decorative candlestick shaped like a dragon. These objects, and the collection of swords and shields in this chamber, call to mind the fact that despite Egypt's national Coptic movement the land was, nevertheless, still part of the Byzantine Empire, and some of the monastic centers enjoyed gifts from the imperial workshops. The two excellent patriarchal crowns, surmounted by the cross and decorated with semi-precious stones, were gifts from the emperor of Ethiopia to the parent Orthodox Coptic church.

Entering chamber P and moving to the left, we find huge iron bolts and keys that once belonged to monastery doors, as well as various utilitarian objects made of metal, including musical instruments and bells. On the other side of the room is an interesting collection of surgical instruments, many of them for use in gynecology and childbirth. They attest to the fact that monastic centers were concerned with the health as well as the spiritual welfare of the neighboring communities.

Chamber Q has a collection of wall paintings from churches in Nubia, primarily from Abd al Nergui and al Sebua. The rest are in the old wing. Most of these paintings were brought to Egypt during the salvage operations in Nubia, during the years 1960 to 1971, when the High Dam was being constructed at Aswan. The Nubian wall paintings can be distinguished from the Coptic in several respects, particularly in the use of muted colors: soft ochers and olive green. Also, the faces tend to be more rounded than the Coptic, and they are painted in flat color. The eyes are usually much too large for the face, and often have a black line underlining the eye-bag. This is one of the largest collections of early Christian wall paintings, which is hardly surprising in view of the fact that Christianity in Nubia survived for eight centuries, and that the largest proportion of Nubia's ancient sites were, in fact, Christian.

We are now back in the chamber with the staircase (J), where several showcases contain manuscripts. Every monastery, indeed possibly every church, once had manuscripts. They were written on sheets of papyrus and sometimes bound into codices, or books. The codex made an appearance in the first century but scrolls existed alongside it for at least two hundred years. In the fourth century the codex took over as the most popular format. Texts on parchment are less common in Egypt, due to the availability and durability of papyrus. There are also texts on ostraca—pieces of broken pottery—as well as on stone, bone, metal, and wooden tablets. All texts were written with reed pens.

The texts include the biographies and teachings of the early anchorites, two leaves from the Gospel of Thomas from Nag Hammadi (see p.22), as well as prayers, sermons, poetry (both religious and profane), magical formulae, and popular romances. The bilingual texts are especially noteworthy. One is a tenth century manuscript from the Fayoum, written in both

Coptic and Arabic, and vividly adorned in the margins with figures of animals and birds. The manuscripts are bound in embossed leather and adorned with miniature paintings of the saints. One of the cabinets contains magical texts with weird symbols. A large number of these have come to light from several sites, along with amulets and some magicians' handbooks written in Greek and demotic, as well as Coptic. The intervention of magical powers was sought in a variety of ways among the pre-Christian communities in the Nile Valley. These included prayers, curses, and rituals that invoked the help of ancient deities. Egyptian amulets, oracles, and spells have been found in all parts of the Mediterranean world and are testimony to the trust placed in magical ritual devised by priests in ancient Egypt, who had a great reputation as healers and magicians.

We now descend the stairs, return to the first chamber (A) and cross to a porch directly opposite. Here there is another collection of funerary stelae that come from various pagan cemeteries throughout Egypt and are believed to date from between the second and fourth centuries. Some of the stelae portray the deceased reclining on a couch holding a bunch of flowers in one hand and a drinking vessel in the other, or standing upright in a temple doorway. Standing figures are frequently shown with arms raised, bent at the elbows; most scholars agree that this is an act of devotion or worship, although there are some who maintain that the gesture can be associated with the hieroglyphic sign for the *ka* (spirit). Certainly, the representation of figures with upraised arms occurs throughout ancient Egyptian history right up to Greco–Roman times, and the resemblance between such figures on Ptolemaic and Roman as well as on Coptic stelae, undoubtedly points to an artistic tradition that developed from the pharaonic period and continued until Coptic times. Another characteristic feature of Egyptian art that may be seen in these stelae is that the legs are frequently sculpted in profile, while the upper part of the body is in full frontal position.

It is interesting to observe that figures in the stelae are frequently flanked by the ancient Egyptian gods Horus and Anubis. Horus, the hawk, was associated with the sun-god and was the son of Osiris the god of the afterlife; Anubis, the jackal, was associated with funeral art from the beginning of Egyptian history. Such figures indicate the perseverance of paganism in cemeteries not far from areas that knew Christianity at an early period.

These stelae are historically important because, although they are the product of rural stone-cutters and are of poor workmanship, they provide evidence of different styles of Coptic writing, idioms, and symbols as well as the names of many towns and villages, and are clear indication that the population of these areas was a mixture of Egyptians and Greeks who lived together.

Old Wing

This wing, which lies to the right of the entrance hall, contains a large collection of woodwork, panel paintings, and pottery. It was closed during and after the war of 1967, when most of the objects were put in storage, and reopened in 1983 after complete renovation of the building. A flight of stairs from the interior garden leads up to the first chamber.

The architectural features of the old wing are worth noting, especially the fine wooden ceilings, arches, and tiles that were all collected from old Coptic houses and placed in the structure of the building. The mashrabiya windows are made of finely carved segments of contrasting woods fixed together without the use of nails or glue, while allowing room between each piece for expansion or contraction of the wood. The building itself and the objects on view are made of a variety of woods. For heavy carpentry sycamore, acacia, palm, and doum were used, and for finer work cedar from Lebanon, pine and walnut from Europe and western Asia, and ebony from Africa were popular.

To the left of chamber 1 is the pinewood altar-dome that was brought from the church of Saint Sergius in Old Cairo. The altar itself is early, dating to the fourth century, but the wooden dome dates to the Fatimid era (tenth to twelfth centuries). The walls of this chamber, as well as those of the next five chambers, are adorned with framed segments of wall paintings that were saved from the churches of Nubia, specifically from Abu al Nergui, Abu al O'da and al Sebua. As already mentioned, these paintings differ from traditional

Coptic wall paintings, especially in the use of muted color. There are two lunettes (paintings in semi-circles) from Bawit, in chamber 4. The left-hand one shows three saints with a horseman to the right, honoring them. The figure to the left is believed to be a martyr. There is also a large painting of Jesus, standing and holding the Bible in one hand while making the sign of the benediction with the other.

We now pass into the section of the museum devoted to a rare collection of assorted woodwork dating from the fourth century to the end of the seventeenth. The sanctuary screen from the church of Saint Barbara in chamber 5 is in sycamore. The panels are carved with biblical scenes including one of Christ and the Virgin with the apostles and another of Christ and Saint Mark.

Many of these wooden objects are of unknown provenance but probably come from various sites in the Fayoum and Middle and Upper Egypt. Although most of them cannot be dated with certainty they have been grouped according to stylistic sequence. The first group of objects, in chamber 6, dates from the fourth to the sixth centuries. They are rectangular and square friezes that may have been placed on coffins as decoration, as they are not large enough for door-lintels. They are carved with Nilotic vegetation like the lotus and papyrus, along with ducks, crocodiles, and Hellenistic mythological subjects, such as Leda and the swan.

Chamber 7 has a cabinet containing wooden panels of the same period, but here the human figure is combined with aquatic plants and animals to form the decorative theme. The most interesting object in this chamber is a large fourth- or fifth-century frieze found on a lintel in the Hanging Church (al Muallaqa). It shows the triumphal entry of Christ (who is portrayed without a beard) into Jerusalem on Palm Sunday, where He is welcomed by a crowd bearing palm fronds. The Greek inscription refers to Him as 'He in whom dwells the fullness of Divinity.'

The second group of objects is in chamber 8. They include wooden panels, which were probably parts of wooden boxes, carved with a wide range of animals and birds—pigeons, peacocks, gazelles, and lambs—as well as religious themes, such as images of the apostles, saints, and Jesus Christ. On the

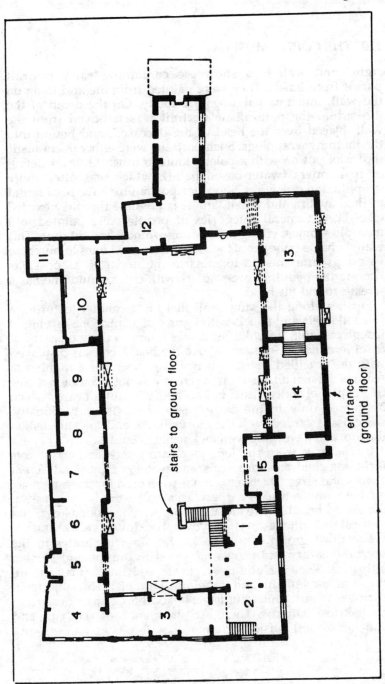

The Coptic Museum: old wing, upper floor

right-hand wall is a showcase containing early portrait panels from Bawit. They were painted from life and hung on the wall, much as paintings are today. On the death of the individual the naturalistic portrait was removed from the wall, placed over the head of the deceased, and bound into the mummy wrappings. Such portraits were either in encaustic (hot wax put on with a palette knife, a brush used for detail) or in tempera (water-based paint), which was often more simplified in execution. Shops for portraiture have been found in the Fayoum and Bawit, and it is possible that they existed elsewhere. General categories of people were painted: old men, old women, young men, young women, and children. This would enable poor people who had lost loved ones to purchase paintings in as near a likeness to the departed as possible. Among the paintings are soldiers with crosses, and one has a wreath round his head.

Further along the same wall there is a cabinet featuring a fine toilet box and panels with figures of saints. One carving of Joseph carrying the child Jesus was found in the monastery of Saint Jeremias at Sakkara. Above the box, a cross is displayed with the crucified Jesus. This is a rare piece, for a number of reasons. First of all, Jesus on the cross was not a common theme in Egypt. Secondly, Jesus is depicted without a beard, which happened only in the early years of Christianity. Finally, the cross is carved with the Horus hawk and the sun disk at the top, and a weeping woman kneeling beneath.

In chamber 9, to the left, there are miscellaneous objects including children's toys, seals, and wooden combs of different shapes and sizes. The larger combs were used for dressing wool for the manufacture of carpets. The seals were for impressing the sacred bread. There are also tongs, large wooden keys, and musical instruments, most of which were found at Sakkara.

The third group of objects in the old wing dates to the seventh century and shows increased Byzantine and Persian influence. They include door panels and lintels that feature the Asian elephant and fabulous animals. The objects in chamber 10 are similar but have, in addition, border designs in geometrical patterns. There are also panels of acrobatic and dancing scenes, musical ceremonies with pipers, dancers, and musicians, as well as hunting scenes, which date to the tenth and eleventh centuries.

The fourth group of objects dates to the Fatimid period. The doors, lintels, and cabinets are in geometric designs of exquisite workmanship. The remarkable taste and skill of Coptic artists was recognized by the Arabs, who recruited the most talented wood-carvers to adorn their mosques. Coptic woodwork differs from Islamic only in the cross as a distinguishing feature.

Finally, the fifth group of objects dates to between the thirteenth and seventeenth centuries. The woodwork is totally devoid of iconographic representations. All the designs are geometric and non-figurative.

Chamber *11* contains patriarchal or episcopal chairs of the tenth century and later. The one to the rear has openwork designs and rosettes carved in relief, with the cross at the center. Chamber *12* is dominated by an ornate carrying-chair. It dates to the seventeenth century and was used for transporting a bride to the church. Also on display is a small door of very fine workmanship. It was executed by Copts but probably for Muslim patrons, as the cross is disguised by carving it at a slant. Such disguising of motifs can be found in mosques, too, where Coptic laborers split the cross motif down the centre of the vertical arm, so that the half cross on each wall would be discernible only to a Copt. The famous fourth-century door of the church of Saint Barbara can also be seen in this chamber. It was brought to the museum by Marcus Simaika to save it from further damage. The bottom part had already been destroyed.

Ascending some stairs, we enter chamber *13*, which contains pottery that has been divided according to decoration and size, not location. The reason for this is that the study of pottery from the Coptic period is still a relatively unexplored field. As in stone and woodwork, textiles and ivorywork, it is possible to trace some Hellenistic as well as Persian and Egyptian symbols. Wild and domestic animals were painted on some of the jars, and the frog, fish, and duck are frequent themes, often combined with vines and tendrils. Egypt had an abundance of raw material for pottery manufacture, including alluvial soil, clay, and sand. It is interesting to note that pottery was so abundant and easy to produce that when cereals and honey were sold, the pottery containers were handed over as well.

Characteristics of Coptic pottery are the burnished surfaces and variety of shapes. For example, some of the plates are divided into segments, for unknown reasons; the ones with circular cavities may be for candles. There are numerous small pots that may have been designed for perfumes and kohl, black eye decoration. One cabinet has a large number of pilgrim flasks, many of which are decorated with the figure of Saint Menas in relief between two kneeling camels. Also on view are the molds for making the flasks. Some of the flasks have the name of the pilgrim written in either Coptic or Greek. The large, finely decorated pottery vessels placed against the walls were collected from monasteries throughout Egypt where they were used for storage.

The remarkable ceilings in this part of the museum should be noted. They were rescued from abandoned Coptic homes in Cairo prior to their demolition, and probably date to the early twentieth century. The central dome is painted with a scene of the port of Istanbul, where the red slanting roofs of the houses are offset by the ships in port.

Another short flight of stairs leads to chamber *14*, which contains numerous pottery fragments with Arabic writing, similar to the pottery sherds of Fustat, the first Arab capital of Egypt, before Cairo. The manufacture of pottery during the eleventh to fifteenth centuries is distinguished by the bright, glazed surfaces with a metallic luster. The pieces are ornamented with floral as well as geometric designs and include Christian motifs such as the fish and the cross. The text (the name of either the owner of the workshop or the man who made the vessel) is in Arabic.

Chamber *15* has a small collection of glassware. The glass industry flourished in Alexandria, Wadi al Natrun, and the Fayoum. Although glass glaze was used in pharaonic times, glass vessels of perfection and beauty only appeared in the eighteenth dynasty (1567–1320 B.C.), perhaps the result of the introduction of western Asian techniques of glass manufacture. Egyptian glass reached a peak of perfection during the early Christian period, when Alexandria became

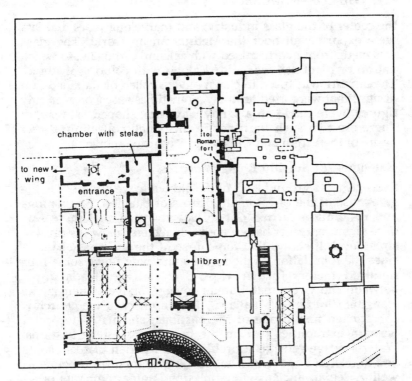

The Coptic Museum (old wing) and the Roman gatehouse

the center of the glass industry, and marvelous vases and jars were exported all over the Mediterranean world. The glass was made from quartz mixed with calcium carbonate, to which natron or plant ash was added along with coloring material. The mixture was fused in clay molds or rolled or flattened into designs that were used for inlay. Sometimes vases, or even tiny figures, were made on a sandy clay core, shaped as desired. There are two such figurines in this small collection: a tiny figure of the Virgin and Child, and a bearded monk.

Gatehouse of the Old Roman Fortress

Descending to ground level of the old wing, we can cross to the gatehouse of the old Roman fortress of Babylon. Excavations and restoration carried out in 1984 revealed that there was once an ancient river harbor about six meters below the present street level. It shows that the course of the river has changed since the foundation of the fortress and now flows some four hundred meters further west. The stairway leads down between the two great Roman towers, above which is the Hanging Church (al Muallaqa). The baptistry of the church is constructed above one of the bastions, and its eastern and western extremities rest on the two southwestern bastions. Water seepage remains a problem but wooden planks enable one to descend and view the Hanging Church from below as well as see an ancient wine-press and some remnants of an early church.

The Library

The library in the old wing has been restored and is now in use for specialist research only, not for the general public. Among its collection of valuable manuscripts are the Nag Hammadi codices.

Center for Coptic Studies

The project to build a modern research facility for an international community of Coptic scholars to the north of the new wing of the Museum has met with some unexpected delays. This is because restoration of the church of Saint Sergius, which flanks the chosen site, was delayed while subsoil water was pumped out of the foundations. Since the water table affects also the site of the Coptic Center, work cannot begin until completion of the restoration project on the church. Meanwhile, specialists in various media are working in the library. They continue to trace stylistic developments of the exhibits in the museum, whose provenance is unknown. The objects in the museum will then be rearranged so as to facilitate an understanding of their historical sequence.

6

COPTIC MONASTERIES

One of the main reasons for the success of the monastic movement in Egypt was that certain religious and philosophical constituents, as well as social conditions, already existed in the land of the Nile that provided a suitable framework for its growth. The ancient Egyptian civilization, as outlined in the *Introduction*, gradually fell prey to successive foreign occupation and there was no leadership in the traditional sense. Yet there was a strong feeling of national identity and personal piety among the people. Their desire for order was a deep-rooted and ancient concept that referred to religious, political, and social as well as cosmic order. Moreover, in ancient Egypt's highly stratified society there had long been a need for, and acceptance of, supervision at different levels under the leadership of an individual who gave a sense of security and spiritual guidance; that was what divine kingship was all about.

Lack of proper leadership in the Roman era, and the imposition of unrealistic tax laws, affected landed farmers and urban dwellers most of all. It was from their ranks that spiritual leaders like Saint Antony and Saint Macarius came. For the great bulk of the Egyptian people, however, especially the soilbound and conservative farmers, religious and ceremonial life in towns and villages hardly changed for the first three centuries of the Christian era. It was only in the fourth century, when paganism was actively suppressed, that their lives were directly affected. The most far-reaching consequence of the official recognition of Christianity as the religion of the Roman Empire was the closing of temples. This resulted in a breakdown of religious ritual and the silencing of oracles. Suddenly people had nowhere to turn. It was this vacuum that was filled by the monastic movement.

When Saint Pachom decided to unify the widespread Christian cenobitic communities and formulate strict rules to govern the daily lives of the monks (see p.26f), he first organized the monks into a hierarchy. He grouped them by activity, according to their talents, thus providing social stratification and leadership within the monasteries. Leading disciplined lives, the monks brought productivity to the soil, revived crafts, and, more importantly, were in communication with non-monastic neighboring communities. There is abundant evidence, in the surviving records of various monasteries, that the monks aided the people economically by providing them with crop surpluses as well as products from monastic craft industries. Although the monks were looked upon as mortals to whom God had given the power of healing, they nevertheless also supplied medication to those who came for a cure. They helped those who sought guidance or blessing, and even played a role as mediators in popular grievances, whether between members of a family or, as was frequent, in disputes over land or water rights between neighbors. In other words, the Pachomian monasteries were not isolated in faraway stretches of the desert but, in many cases, were within easy reach of the valley settlements.

The hard business of survival in desert conditions in Egypt has been somewhat exaggerated. Although there is evidence of tens of thousands of anchorites living in the desert, archaeological evidence shows that the caves were often ancient tombs flanking the fertile floodplain, or else were situated near oases in the western desert or located in areas where there were natural springs. Monasteries that were near populated areas provided a restored priesthood which, in a country so much given to religious ritual as Egypt, was extremely important. This is not to say that a monastery was regarded as serving the same function as a temple, but merely that it provided a new focus for worship. Nor did prayers to ancient gods come to an end: "I was the son of a pagan priest," wrote a Copt in the Theban area in the fifth century, "and as a child I watched my father making sacrifice."

The Coptic Monastic Sites of Egypt

Northern Egypt

Shrine of Saint Menas, Maryut   (p.120)
Monastery of Saint Dimiana, Mansura   (p.56)
Kellia, ancient monastic site   (p.126)
Wadi al Natrun (Desert of Scetis)   (p.122)
*Monastery of Saint Macarius   (p.122)
*Monastery of the Syrians   (p.124)
*Monastery of Saint Bishai   (p.125)
*Monastery of the Romans   (p.125)

In and around Cairo

*Convent of Saint George   (p.89)
*Convent of Saint Mercurius   (p.89)
Monastery of Saint Menas   (p.92)
*Monastery of Saint Mercurius, Tamouh, Giza   (p.59)

The Red Sea

*Monastery of Saint Antony   (p.127)
*Monastery of Saint Paul   (p.129)

* functioning, with resident monks or nuns

The Fayoum and Beni Suef

*Monastery of al Azab (p.130)
*Monastery of the Angel Gabriel (p.130)
*Monastery of Saint Samuel
*Monastery of Saint Antony, Beni Suef (p.132)
*Monastery of al Maimun, Beni Suef (p.132)
*Convent of the Holy Virgin, Bayad (p.58)

Middle and Upper Egypt

Gebel al Tair, Samalut (p.55)
*Monastery of Saint Mary (Durunka), Asyut (p.55)
*Monastery of Saint Mary (al Muharraq), Qusiya (p.56)
Monastery of Saint Thomas, Sidfa (p.134)
*White Monastery, Sohag (p.134)
Red Monastery, Sohag (p.135)
Monastery of the Martyrs, Akhmim (p.57)
Convent of the Holy Virgin, Akhmim (p.58)
*Monastery of Saint Palomen, Nag Hammadi (p.135)
Monastery of Saint Theodore, Luxor (p.137)
Convent of Saint George, Esna (p.137)
Convent of the Holy Martyrs, Esna (p.57)
Monastery of Saint Pachom, Edfu (p.137)
Monastery of Saint Simeon, Aswan (p.138)

Kharga Oasis

Necropolis of Bagawat (p.139)

Although cenobitic Pachomian monasticism spread rapidly, large ascetic communities that grew up around spiritual leaders like Saint Antony in the eastern desert and Saint Macarius in Wadi al Natrun were, based on architectural and archaeological considerations, semi-cenobitic. The monks met once a week only for mass and a communal meal, followed by a meeting at which work was allocated for the forthcoming week. The rest of the time the monks could return to their cells or caves to pray or work alone. Saint Pjol, founder of the White Monastery at Sohag, modified Pachom's rules and introduced a few of his own, such as allowing two monks to share a cell, so that each could report on the pious behavior of the other.

Monasteries of Northern Egypt

Shrine of Saint Menas (Abu Mina)

The fabled city of Saint Menas is situated in Maryut (Mareotis), which lies in the desert southwest of Alexandria. It was one of the great centers of pilgrimage during the fifth to seventh centuries, famous as a place of healing. Thousands of people came from all over the Christian world, and took home with them sacred water in tiny pottery ampules shaped like a flat, two-handled jug and stamped with the figure of the saint between two camels.

Although the site lost its widespread importance after the Arab conquest, the city of Saint Menas was described in glowing terms by an Arab geographer, al Bakri, in the eleventh century, and also by numerous medieval historians and pilgrims. They wrote of superb buildings decorated with statues and mosaics, situated in a fertile region with vineyards. Numerous modern scholars went in search of the site, but despite clues provided in the medieval writings, all trace of the 'city' was lost. It was thought to be legendary until, in 1905, it was discovered by German archaeologist Carl Maria Kaufmann. At first it was not clear that the ruined site he excavated was, in fact, the city of Menas. Discovery of the tomb of the saint, however, dispelled all doubt. Thirty marble stairs led down to a crypt, and the tomb of Saint Menas lay some ten meters beneath the high altar of the ruins of the original church. In the tomb was an icon of the saint exactly as al Bakri had described it: a Roman officer standing between two kneeling camels. The excavators also found a potter's workshop where souvenir objects including jugs, lamps, and flasks had been fired 1,500 years earlier for sale to pilgrims.

Saint Menas is said to have suffered martyrdom in 296, when the soles of his feet were torn off, his eyes were gouged, and his tongue was dragged out by the roots. Despite these terrible mutilations, Menas was yet able to stand up and address spectators. Finally, the emperor himself slew him and set his body adrift on the Mediterranean in an iron coffin. This is said to have been cast ashore and loaded onto a camel by some passing Bedouins. They proceeded with it into the desert but when the camel reached a certain point, it refused to move further. It was there that the coffin with the body of Saint Menas was buried.

The basilica constructed over the burial place of the saint has been attributed to the emperor Arcadius (395–408). The builders spared nothing in its construction. Subsequent emperors erected a second building, and a great cathedral was built over the crypt.

After the Arab conquest and the Byzantine withdrawal from Egypt, the shrine of Saint Menas was in the hands of the Greek Orthodox church. During subsequent disputes between the Greek Orthodox and the Coptic Orthodox churches on the question of jurisdiction, the site was pillaged and the stone, including valuable marble, was taken for reuse elsewhere. In the eighth century the government decreed that the shrine belonged to the Coptic Orthodox church.

The Coptic community of Egypt is anxious to resurrect the ancient glory of the city of Saint Menas. In 1959, under the patriarchate of Kirollos VI, a foundation stone for a new monastery was laid, and subsequent progress on the site, though slow, has been significant. Meanwhile, archaeologists digging along the northern coast prior to the construction of a highway leading to the sacred site have made several important discoveries in recent years. One is a monastic center comprising a main church and a large number of cells, along with two tombs. This site provides evidence that the monks of the holy city of Saint Menas may have lived in urban, rather than isolated communities.

Monasteries of Wadi al Natrun

The famous monasteries of Wadi al Natrun lie in a long, narrow desert depression twenty-five meters below sea level, southwest of the resthouse between Cairo and Alexandria. The name Wadi (valley) al Natrun (natron) refers to the vast quantities of sodium hydroxide obtained from the lakes here. It was used in ancient times for mummification purposes and in Roman times for glass manufacture.

Wadi al Natrun, or the Desert of Scetis as it was known in the early Christian period, was one of the most famous Christian sites in the fourth and fifth centuries. Two of the famous names associated with it are Saint Amon and Saint Macarius the Great. Both were inspired by Antonian monasticism and became great spiritual leaders. The Desert of Scetis was also, according to Coptic tradition, one of the sites visited by the Holy Family during the Flight into Egypt.

Because of its isolation, Wadi al Natrun became the official residence of the Coptic patriarch for many years, and the number of monasteries grew until there were reputedly one hundred in the area. A great deal of church literature was translated into the northern Bohairic dialect of Coptic by the monks here, and the reputation for linguistics they thus gained remains to this day.

The monasteries of Wadi al Natrun were hardest hit of all by the plague in the middle of the fourteenth century and this, combined with frequent Bedouin raids, resulted in a sudden decline in the population. Al Maqrizi recorded that in the fifteenth century seven monasteries survived in the area. Today there are only four. They can be visited in a single day.

Monastery of Saint Macarius (Abu Maqar)

Saint Macarius the Great (Abu Maqar), the son of a village priest and disciple of Saint Antony, with whom he lived for many years near the Red Sea, decided to adopt a life of contemplation and prayer around the year 330. The caves in the depression of Wadi al Natrun were already inhabited by a large number of ascetics and he, too, lived in a cave. As a result of a divine revelation, however, Macarius built a church that became the focus of the community. The monastery of Saint Macarius acquired great distinction in the sixth century when it became the official residence of the Coptic patriarchs. In fact, it takes pride in having supplied no less than thirty patriarchs from its ranks, more than any other monastery in Egypt. In 1970 the spiritual leader Abuna Matta al Maskin (Father Matthew the Poor One), who revived the anchoritic spirit when he and some of his followers took to caves in the Wadi al Rayan area of the Fayoum, settled in Wadi al Natrun with a group of hermits. They at first constructed cells outside the walls of the monastery of Saint Macarius, but now live inside.

The churches in the monastery have been destroyed and rebuilt many times in their long history, and renovations continue even today. The main church is dedicated to Saint Benjamin and Saint John the Baptist. A second church was built in honor of the forty-nine martyrs who were buried on the site; it contains icons of the three Macarii, Saint Macarius, Saint Mark, and Saint George, as well as the Holy Virgin. The church of the Forty-Nine Martyrs is used for the liturgy during some Coptic celebrations, including the feast of the Nativity. This is the occasion when the relics of the three Macarii, and also those of Saint John the Short, are transferred from the church of Saint Macarius to be placed near the transept of the church of the Forty-Nine Martyrs.

The fortress or keep (*qasr* in Arabic) is a three-storied tower. In such towers, which were always constructed near a natural well or spring, the monks could protect themselves when under siege by Bedouins. Storage space was usually on the first floor, sleeping accommodation on the second, and a chapel, sometimes several, on the third. The keep in the monastery of Saint Macarius is entered by means of a narrow drawbridge. It has numerous chapels and churches. The one on the first floor, dedicated to the Holy Virgin, has a fine thirteenth-century screen. The second floor has chapels dedicated to Saint Michael and to Saints Antony, Paul, and Pachom. On the third floor there is a church dedicated to anchorites, in which nine local hermits are painted on the walls.

Today the monks of the monastery of Saint Macarius collaborate with engineers, agronomists, and scientists at nearby Sadat City. They have a modern pump and pump-house as well as tractors. The monastery has thriving agriculture on reclaimed land as well as palm and olive groves. There are about one hundred monks in residence. This is Pachomian monasticism at its finest: pious men with vision and education, combining a life of contemplation and prayer with discipline.

Monastery of the Syrians (al Suryan)

More correctly called the monastery of Saint Mary, this is one of the leading monasteries of the Wadi al Natrun. It was purchased by Syrian merchants at the beginning of the eighth century for the use of Syrian monks. By the eleventh century the monastery could boast of sixty monks. After the plague, which took a terrible toll, the monastery was reinhabited in the fifteenth century by Syrian and Coptic monks, with the latter element predominant.

The library of the monastery contains over three thousand valuable books and hundreds of manuscripts, housed in a special building within the complex. Also, a museum contains icons dating to the sixteenth and seventeenth centuries and a twelfth-century marble tray from Nubia.

The main church, on the site of the cave of Saint Bishoi (which can still be visited), is dedicated to the Holy Virgin and dates to the tenth century. The basin for the foot-washing rite of Maundy Thursday, which is usually located at the entrance of a church, is in the middle of the nave. The sanctuary doors are made of wood and inlaid ivory of particularly fine workmanship. The two central panels of the choir door show Christ and the Virgin. The other panels feature Coptic and Syrian patriarchs as well as Saint Mark the Evangelist and Saint Ignatius, bishop of Antioch. The altar of the church is a slab of black marble that may have been imported by Syrian monks. One of the most important and unusual paintings is in the southern apse. It is a composition of the Annunciation and the Nativity with no separation between the two scenes; the theme of the life of the Virgin, ending with the Assumption, is continued in the other domes.

This church is used during the summer for the celebration of the divine liturgy. During the winter months the monks hold the service in the church of the Lady Mary, sometimes called the Cave Church, which is one of several lying to the northeast of the monastery.

The monastery owns farmland to the northeast and the monks are also active in animal husbandry. Lying between the monastery and the agricultural land is a resthouse where church groups and students are welcome. The monastery is closed to the public during certain feasts.

Monastery of Saint Bishai

The monastery of Saint Bishai, like the monastery of the Syrians, restricts visitors during certain times of the year. The monastery is named after its patron saint, who went to Wadi al Natrun around the beginning of the fifth century after a divine revelation and joined the hermit Saint John the Short. The latter had lived alone for many years and suggested that Bishai do likewise, which he did. During the doctrinal disputes between the Melkite and monophysite monks, both Saint John the Short and Saint Bishai sought refuge with ascetic communities in the area of the Fayoum. In fact, Saint Bishai died in the Fayoum and the monastery in Wadi al Natrun that bears his name was only constructed in the seventh century. It contains four churches in addition to the main one built in honor of the patron saint. Saint Bishai's relics were taken there in the ninth century.

Monastery of the Romans (al Baramus)

This is the northernmost of the four monasteries of Wadi al Natrun. It is named after Saints Maximus and Domitius, Roman brothers who sought the spiritual guidance of Saint Macarius after having served in the Roman army in Syria. The two brothers died a few days apart, and Saint Macarius dedicated the cave in which they lived to their memory and built a church near the site. Today the monastery contains five churches: that of the Holy Virgin, that of Saint Theodore, that of Saint George, that of Saint John the Baptist, and that of Saint Michael, which is situated on the second floor of the keep. The keep has a drawbridge, secured by what is known as an Egyptian lock: pins that slip into position and which can be lifted by a large wooden key. The refectory, which is not used today, is near the entrance of the main church. The refectory table is a remarkable structure some six meters in length that appears to have been carved out of solid rock. Within this cell-like chamber, hermits and monks once shared their weekly meal. Leading off the refectory is the baptistry and a press for making sacramental oil from olives.

The monasteries of Wadi al Natrun are large, self-supporting communities that are today enjoying a revival and undergoing expansion. The monks, many of whom are university graduates, are experimenting with agriculture and animal husbandry, introducing new crops and breeds of cattle. They also encourage the development of small craft industries like weaving and glass manufacturing, which are springing up anew in the area. Over twenty thousand people in the town of Wadi al Natrun, and thousands more in the surrounding rural villages, turn to the monks for spiritual guidance.

Kellia

An ancient site mentioned in many early writings on monasticism, Kellia is situated in the western Delta, some twenty kilometers east of the Gianaclis vineyards. Its name is derived from the Greek word for 'cells.' According to tradition, the site was first occupied when the monks at Wadi al Natrun had become so numerous that they sought a new colony. Apparently two abbots, Amon and Antony, took their usual evening meal at the ninth hour (3 p.m.), and then journeyed eastwards into the desert until sunset. They marked with a cross the place they had reached, and then proceeded to construct their respective cells out of sight and hearing of one another. Others monks followed, until the cells extended over an area eleven kilometers long.

A joint Franco–Swiss archaeological mission has been excavating the site since 1965, and their work has brought to light a great deal of valuable information on the growth and development of a semi-cenobitic monastic life in Egypt. The cells, for example, are not the expected single chambers, but comprise a number of rooms, suggesting that the monks did not, like the founders of the community, seek absolute seclusion. Most of them shared living quarters, and the individual cells have decorated niches for books or utilitarian objects such as pots, plates, and jars. Each group of cells seems to have had a small garden for vegetables. Current excavation has been accelerated in recent years because of the threat from urban and agricultural expansion, as well as from subsoil water.

Monasteries of the Red Sea

The monasteries of Saint Antony and Saint Paul, on the Gulf of Suez, can be visited in a single day and permission is not normally required. Women should wear skirts and preferably a head covering. At Saint Antony's monastery guests are graciously received, though if accommodation is required, a letter of introduction from the Coptic patriarchate in Cairo is needed. There is now a new guest wing for visitors, and simple but substantial meals are provided twice a day. In return for this hospitality guests may leave donations, and gifts such as tea, sugar, rice, or flour are always welcome. At the monastery of Saint Paul, accommodation is provided within the monastery for men only. Women are accommodated at a guest lodge outside the monastery walls. Permission from the patriarchate in Cairo is needed only if more than one night's accommodation is required.

Monastery of Saint Antony

The famous monastery of Saint Antony lies some 130 kilometers southeast of Cairo, near Zaafarana on the Red Sea coast. It is approached from the desert road that branches off from the Nile Valley at al Burumbul, or from the road leading from Suez. It is well supplied with sweet water from three springs and is at present inhabited by about fifty monks.

Saint Antony was born in the village of Koma (Kom al Arus) in Middle Egypt towards the middle of the third century, and he is said to have died at the age of 105. His parents were fairly well-to-do, but as a result of visionary inspiration, he sold his inheritance and gave his money to the poor; he then retreated to the cliffs flanking the Nile Valley, before eventually settling beneath a range of mountains near the Red Sea known today as the South Qalala (Mount Clysma in

Roman times). He became the spiritual leader of a large number of hermits; his was a semi-cenobitic form of monasticism with the monks meeting only once a week for mass and a communal meal, followed by a formal gathering at which work was allocated for the rest of the week. The hermits were otherwise free to return to their cells or caves or to work alone. As Antony's reputation grew, more and more ascetics gravitated towards him and he was obliged to take refuge in a cave 270 meters above the present monastery—680 meters above sea level.

The monastery of Saint Antony was founded in the fourth century, a few years after the death of the saint, when his followers settled down in the area where their master had lived. It is said that around the year 790 Coptic monks from Wadi al Natrun, who had sought refuge at Saint Antony's monastery during the factional disputes with the Melkites in the fifth century, disguised themselves as Bedouins, entered the monastery and removed the remains of Saint John the Short to take back to Wadi al Natrun with them. There were frequent Bedouin raids in the eighth and ninth centuries in which the monastery was severely damaged and a great many monks lost their lives. Its history thereafter is uncertain until the twelfth century, when the monastery was rebuilt and adorned with specially commissioned works of art, particularly in the church of Saint Antony. The monastery was again partly destroyed by Bedouin tribes in the fifteenth century, when the library was burned, and it was not reoccupied until the end of the sixteenth century when, under the patriarch Gabriel VII, monks from Wadi al Natrun helped restore the buildings.

This is one of the most beautiful monasteries in Egypt, largely because of its setting. It nestles beneath the rugged mountains along the Red Sea coast and is surrounded by high walls of modern construction, over ten meters high in some places. The thickness of the walls provides sentry walks around the top, and there are several watch towers. The guardroom over the gateway has a trap door that was once the only means of access to the monastery; visitors and supplies were hoisted with the aid of a pulley. Today the main gate is used.

The oldest part of the monastery is the church of Saint Antony, which is built over his tomb. The wall paintings in the narthex and nave are from the twelfth or thirteenth century and include Saint George on horseback and a well-preserved painting of three of the Desert Fathers. Regarded as fine examples of medieval Coptic art, they have recently been restored by the Byzantine Institute of Archaeology.

The cave in which Antony took refuge from the thousands of people who came to see him is not visible from the monastery itself. The steep climb is worthwhile as the site commands a magnificent view of the surrounding mountainscape. Antony's cave was situated at the end of a narrow tunnel, approached from a ledge. Below the ledge, a small terrace is said to be the place where he used to sit and weave baskets from palm leaves. He was kept supplied with provisions by his disciples who came frequently to visit him. The walls of the cave are covered with graffiti, most of which date to medieval times. There are also two panel paintings, one of Christ and one of Saint Antony.

Monastery of Saint Paul

The monastery of Saint Paul lies about twenty kilometers south of Zaafarana on the Red Sea coast. A signpost marks the road that leads through a twisting and rugged mountainscape towards the secluded haven. Saint Paul was older than Saint Antony, who, according to tradition, came to bury him. Unfortunately, little was written of Paul in early Coptic sources. He is believed to have retired to the desert at the age of sixteen to escape the persecutions of Decius. The monastery was founded at the end of the fifth or early sixth century, abandoned in the fifteenth century, and only recolonized in the seventeenth century.

The monastery is compact, rectangular in shape and surrounded by high walls. Visitors originally gained entrance by means of a pulley, which can still be seen. Today visitors use a gateway from the south, entering a picturesque village community with fields and domestic animals, mills and a bakery. The monastic buildings are concentrated around the cave where the hermit is believed to have lived in seclusion for eighty years. The church of Saint Paul was built over this cave, where his remains are buried. The wall paintings date to the beginning of the eighteenth century. In one of them, the Holy Virgin, flanked by angels, holds Jesus. Another shows an archangel protecting the three youths in the furnace. All the figures are frontal and the execution of the work is naive and typically Coptic in spirit. The other three churches in the monastery are dedicated to Saint Mercurius, the Holy Virgin, and Saint Michael. The latter is the largest and dates to the seventeenth century.

The water that supplies the monastery comes from 'Saint Paul's Spring,' which emerges from a crevice in the rock and flows into a cement basin. This, in turn, flows into another basin situated a few meters away. The first basin is used for drinking and cooking, the second for washing, and a third channels the water for irrigating the vegetable gardens, as well as tiny palm groves and an olive plantation.

Monasteries of the Fayoum and Beni Suef

Monasticism was established in the Fayoum in the fifth and sixth centuries, and records indicate that the number of monasteries reached thirty-five throughout the province and vicinity. Today there are two monastic sites that have resident monks, and the monasteries are undergoing expansion.

Monastery of al Azab

The monastery of al Azab, best approached from the road to Beni Suef, is most popular among the inhabitants of the Fayoum, probably because it is the burial place of the much loved bishop of the Fayoum and Giza, Anba Abram, who died in 1914. The monastery was inhabited from the twelfth to the eighteenth centuries. Now restored and repopulated with resident monks, it attracts a large number of pilgrims during the mulid in commemoration of the Assumption of the Virgin, which is celebrated betweeen August 15 and 22 each year.

Monastery of the Angel Gabriel (al Malak)

Another monastic site in the Fayoum that has been reimbued with vigor is the monastery of the Angel Gabriel at Naqlun.

*Inside the monastery of Saint Paul, Red Sea.
Photograph by Cassandra Vivian.*

The monastery, which might date to as early as the seventh century, was rebuilt and redecorated at the beginning of this century, and again in the last few years. It stands beneath a hollow in the mountain and draws its water from the canal of al Manhi. In the neighborhood are large numbers of cells in the form of caves, which were once inhabited by members of the semi-cenobitic community of the Fayoum. The annual festival in this monastery is in remembrance of the time Jacob sought shade in the hollow in the mountain above it. Pilgrims to the monastery inhabit the many dwelling places that have been built around the main church of Saint Gabriel.

Monastery of Saint Antony

In the area of Beni Suef, some 120 kilometers south of Cairo on the western bank of the Nile, there are numerous functioning monasteries. The most important is the monastery of Saint Antony, near the town of Bush. It was built on property which, according to tradition, was owned by the father of Saint Antony. The church of Saint Antony within the monastery was built towards the end of the nineteenth century, and has recently undergone considerable renovation.

Monastery of al Maimun

The monastery of al Maimun, situated on the eastern bank of the Nile at Beni Suef, was visited and described by many medieval travelers, but seems not to have been inhabited after the thirteenth century. Its restoration and reoccupation today are, consequently, part of the historical record. Within the monastery are two fine churches which have now been restored.

Monasteries of Middle and Upper Egypt

Middle Egypt was once inhabited by thousands of hermits who lived in ancient tombs built in the mountain ranges bordering the floodplain or founded monasteries within reach of the cultivable land. The cave-dwelling hermits may strike a reader as unusual, but it is quite likely that many people, whole families in fact, lived in caves at various times, and for

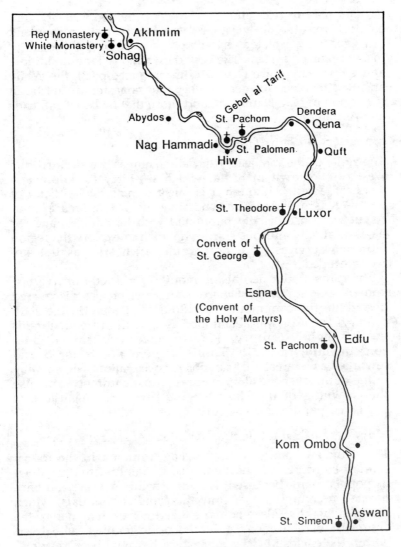

The monasteries of Upper Egypt

various reasons. Certainly, the caves provided security, and comfort from the hot weather. With the monastic movement, however, such isolated cave-dwellers were brought together in an organized system. The best known monasteries in Middle and Upper Egypt are Deir al Muharraq (see p.56), the White and Red monasteries near Sohag, the monasteries that lie in the region of Nag Hammadi, and those that lie between Luxor and Aswan.

Monastery of Saint Thomas

The ruins of the monastery of Saint Thomas are situated due west of the town of Sidfa, which is thirty-six kilometers south of Asyut. Although it is fairly remote and difficult of access, it is described here because the whole area around Asyut was once heavily populated with hermitages, and for those of an adventurous spirit who wish to explore the region with the services of a local guide, such sites as this are recommended.

The ruins are located at the mouth of a dried-out riverbed known as Wadi Sarga, where a manuscript was discovered describing the community that flourished there in the sixth century. The area was abandoned as a result of frequent raids in the eighth century. It was never reoccupied and, consequently, the wall paintings were not restored and reworked as in areas that saw longer occupation. The painting in the dome over the altar features Christ enthroned and also the crowning of the Holy Virgin. This is among the best preserved paintings in the early Coptic tradition.

Monastery of Saint Shenuda (White Monastery)

This famous monastery near Sohag, founded in the fourth century by Saint Pjol and dedicated to Saint Shenuda, gained its popular name because it is built of white limestone. It once boasted a community of four thousand individuals, which dropped by the 1970s to no more than four resident monks; the churches were used by several Coptic families who lived within the enclosure. The monastery has now been restored, the people have been relocated, and monks have taken up residence.

The monastery is best approached from the Nile Valley south of Sohag. From a distance, it closely resembles an Egyptian temple with its sloping walls like an ancient pylon. The church of Saint Shenuda occupies the largest part of the monastery. It is a fine church with a three-aisled nave and a gallery with free-standing columns, which frame niches that are hollowed out in the semi-circular apses. The main body of the church is decorated with columns surmounted by architraves forming more niches. The deeply cut stonework is characteristic of the fifth century. The church's three vaulted apses are made of fired brick and dedicated to Saint Shenuda (center), Saint George, and the Virgin Mary.

Monastery of Saint Bishai (Red Monastery)

The monastery of Saint Bishai is built of burnt brick, and is smaller than the White Monastery of Saint Shenuda three kilometers to the south. It was built at the edge of the cultivated land but is today in the midst of the village. Like the monastery of Saint Shenuda, it is characterized by great simplicity. Saint Bishai once had three thousand monks under him, but the number of monks at the monastery dwindled, and by the 1970s there were none. What were once the narthex and nave of the church are today occupied by several structures of modern date.

The chapel of the Blessed Virgin, in the southeastern corner, may have been the oldest part of the monastery. But the part of the monastery frequently visited and commented on in medieval times was the church of the patron saint. It is situated at the northeastern corner and seems to have had many features in common with the church of Saint Shenuda in the White Monastery: the nave and side aisles surmounted by architraves and columns forming niches above, and apses adorned with beautiful wall paintings. The icons on the sanctuary screen are of Saint Shenuda, Saint Bishai, and Saint Pjol.

Monastery of Saint Palomen

This monastery—which is today no more than a group of churches, none of which is ancient—is situated near Hiw, south of Nag Hammadi. It lies within a semicircle of land about five kilometers in diameter created by the Nile describing a course to the south and then west, before resuming its flow to the northwest. The area is an extremely fertile and picturesque one, where Christians are numerous to this day.

The monastery can be seen from a distance, its bell-tower with latticed walls rising above the surrounding agricultural land. Within the monastery are three churches, dedicated to Saint Mercurius, Saint Palomen, and Saint Dimiana. The church of Saint Dimiana is constructed a meter and a half below the level of the rest of the monastery and is believed to be the most ancient part of the building, but its date is unknown.

Saint Palomen (Anba Balamun) was one of the earliest anchorites in Upper Egypt. He was the ascetic who served as a model for Saint Pachom, founder of Pachomian monasticism. The cave of Saint Palomen, whose mulid or annual celebration in his honor is still observed, is located in an isolated stretch of desert to the east. This saint was said to have died from excessive fasting, and such abstinence may have been one of the reasons why Pachom, when he left the monastery to found one of his own, set down a strict rule to ensure the health as well as the spiritual well-being of his followers.

To the north, beyond the verdure of the valley, rises the Gebel al Tarif. This range of hills blocks off the horizon from west to east, and it was here that the famous Gnostic codices of Nag Hammadi were discovered in 1947. According to one account, a huge boulder had fallen off a slope, revealing a jar that was found by peasant farmers. In another account, two brothers chanced upon the jars while they were digging for fertilizer. The codices were believed to have been hidden when the Byzantine church stamped out what they regarded as heretical groups, around the year 400. The proximity of two cenobitic communities, one Coptic (distinguished by strict orthodoxy of doctrine) and the other Gnostic, with its wide range of religious traditions, is interesting; they were undoubtedly aware of one another and, in fact, the Gnostic literature was translated into Coptic. There may have been strife between the two communities, a suggestion that is supported by a decree issued by Theodore, who succeeded Pachom in 367; he declared that the thirty-ninth letter of

Saint Athanasius should be translated into Coptic and read throughout the monasteries of the country. This letter was highly critical of the books written by the Gnostics, "to which," he wrote, "they attribute antiquity and give the names of saints."

The Gnostic movement (see *Chapter One*) was extremely popular until suppressed by its enemies in the fourth century. It is possible that Egyptian monasticism in its stabilized form under Saint Pachom arose, in part, out of response to the Gnostics, who were cenobitic.

Monasteries in Luxor

Many ancient Egyptian monuments were converted into monastic centers in the fourth and fifth centuries, especially in the area of Luxor. The ancient Egyptian temples known as Deir al Madina and Deir al Bahari on the Theban necropolis are two of the best known examples. The monastery of Saint Theodore (Tadrus), southwest of the temple of Madinet Habu, is less well known but easily accessible. It is a small monastery with one church, and most of the religious pictures are of modern date. It is dedicated to one of Egypt's most popular warrior-saints, Theodore, according to Coptic tradition a general who was tortured and suffered martyrdom during the Diocletian persecutions.

Convent of Saint George

The convent of Saint George (Mari Girgis), situated about halfway between Luxor and Esna, is a large and impressive structure surrounded by a two-meter-high wall. The main church has twenty-one domes and six haikals with altars. The latter are dedicated to Saint Pachom, Saint Mercurius, the Blessed Virgin, Saint George, Saint Paul the Theban, and Saint Michael.

The annual festival in honor of Saint George is held in mid-November, when thousands of pilgrims travel to the area, and the bishop of Luxor takes up residence in one of the guestrooms.

Monastery of Saint Pachom

The monastery of Saint Pachom (Anba Bakhum al Shayib) is situated in the western desert, seven kilometers west of Edfu.

Surrounded by walls, the main church in the enclosure, dedicated to the saint, comprises four haikals with altars. Although the icons are not of very impressive quality, the site is nevertheless convenient to visit because of its proximity to the famous temple of Horus at Edfu.

Monastery of Saint Simeon

There are two monasteries that bear the name of Saint Simeon in Aswan. One is a functioning monastery whose resident monks are active in the community. The other, no longer occupied, is an archaeological site that lies on the west bank of the Nile, opposite Aswan. This is dedicated to a local saints who lived there in the fifth century. Of its origins we know little. The present construction dates to the seventh century. There is evidence of restoration in the tenth century, but the monastery was abandoned in the thirteenth century for unknown reasons. Lack of water or danger from roving bands of nomads have been suggested as possible causes.

The surrounding wall is over six meters high. The upper part is of sun-dried brick and the lower courses, of hewn stone, are sunk into the rock. At intervals along the wall there are towers. Indeed, the monastery may originally have been a Roman fortress, taken over by the monks and transformed into a monastery.

The cliff face divides the monastery into an upper and a lower level from north to south. The entrance, to the east, leads to the lower level. It has a vaulted central corridor; on the eastern wall is a painting of Christ enthroned with the archangel Michael, flanked by six apostles. The small chambers on each side of the corridor contained from six to eight beds for the monks. The upper level, approached by a staircase in the southern angle, is similarly arranged; monks once lived in cells opening out on each side of the corridor. At the northern end of the upper level is the main building, which itself is double-storied. The church lies to the southeast between the building and the outer wall. The roof was originally a series of domes supported by square pillars. The domed apse at the east has a well-preserved painting of enthroned Christ, His hand raised in benediction. He is flanked by four angels, two of which have wings, long hair, and splendid robes. On either side of the recesses are seven seated figures. A cave leading off the northwest corner of the chapel is believed to have been the dwelling place of the patron saint. It has painted walls and a decorated ceiling.

The northern wall of the upper level of the monastery is built over the enclosure wall, with windows looking over the steep cliff. Below the main building are some rock-hewn cells and a rock-chapel painted with saints.

Kharga Oasis

Necropolis of Bagawat

Distant Kharga oasis was once a remote area where hermits sought seclusion to pursue their ascetic lives, and to which the great Christian theologian Saint Athanasius was banished during the controversies of the fourth century.

The main church of the sprawling necropolis, which is some five hundred meters long and two hundred meters in breadth, stands near its center. Thought to date to the fifth century, this church is one of the most ancient in Egypt. Around it are over 250 chapels of sun-dried brick, built between the third and the seventh centuries.

The chapel of the Exodus is of special interest. Its paintings may be attributed to the fourth century, and it has different scenes from the Old Testament somewhat crudely painted around the circular walls. They include the Exodus, Noah's ark, Adam and Eve, Daniel in the lion's den, and Abraham's sacrifice. One painting of Jonah being thrown to the whale also shows him being rejected by the whale.

Another chapel is known both as the chapel of Peace and as the Byzantine Tomb, because its walls are painted with subject matter similar in style to that of the catacombs of Alexandria. It shows an admixture of ancient Egyptian ritual and Christian themes. One painting is a representation of Saints Paul and Takla Hamanout, who seem to have been popular in Kharga.

EPILOGUE

A highly religious society does not suddenly change. We are dealing with a very old world in which, in the words of Peter Brown in *The Making of Late Antiquity*, "changes did not come as disturbing visitations from outside; they happened all the more forcibly for having been pieced together from ancient and familiar materials." This was doubtless the reason for the rapid spread of Christianity in Egypt, the success of the monastic movement, and the widespread reverence for the Holy Family.

Devotion to patron saints, especially through their relics, has continued through the ages. Both the sanctifying of revered people, and the transference of parts of their bodies from site to site, are part of an ancient pattern of ritual in the Nile Valley that lingered on in the new Christian setting. The transference of revered objects from one place to another has its parallel in ancient times. In the monastery of Saint Macarius in Wadi al Natrun, the monks move from the church of Saint Macarius to the church of the Forty-Nine Martyrs during the winter, and take with them the relics of the three Macarii and Saint John the Short; whenever the divine liturgy is celebrated, it is in the presence of the relics of the saints. In ancient Egypt, during festivals like the annual feast of Opet in Luxor, the sacred statue of the deity was borne in procession from Luxor temple to Karnak at the height of the flood, so that at each place, a 'presence' was felt.

One of the reasons why Saint Menas holds a special place in the hearts of the Coptic community may be that many of the miracles that he was said to have performed—thirteen in

140

number—closely resemble the popular ancient myth of Osiris: Saint Menas was said, for example, to have restored to life a man who had been cut to pieces by desert tribes, and also to have joined up the parts of the body of an unfortunate man who had been chewed by a crocodile. The joining together of the parts of a dismembered body is reminiscent of what happened to Osiris, whose body had furthermore, like that of Menas, been sealed in a coffin and cast on water.

This is not to suggest that there is any direct link between Osiris and Menas. It merely shows that a tradition does not die if it is meaningful to a community. Although the revealed Christian truth differs from paganism, there is little doubt that Christianity took hold in Egypt because it shared many characteristics with the mystery cults, especially in the central mystery, the resurrection of the body, and the afterlife. Egyptians embraced Christianity because it gave them familiar altars, priesthoods, a heavenly hierarchy of angels, and God as the father and fashioner of order. The doctrine of future rewards and punishments had its origins in the distant past, in the 'negative confession' before Osiris, when the deceased swore that they had never failed to lead an exemplary life, and were judged accordingly. The efficacy of prayer, forgiveness of sins, and the rite of baptism or purification with water, existed in Egypt for thousands of years before the Christian era. Finally, it is interesting to note that the Coptic church is the only church that confers ordination not by imposition of hands but by the act of breathing; this, too, is a long-standing tradition in Egypt; the expression 'giving the breath of life' was a common one in ancient Egyptian texts.

SELECTED BIBLIOGRAPHY

Abbott, N. *The Monasteries of the Fayoum*. University of Chicago Press, 1937.

Aldred, Cyril. *Egyptian Art in the Days of the Pharaohs*. Thames and Hudson, London, 1980.

Badawy, Alexander. *Coptic Art and Archaeology*. MIT Press, Cambridge, Mass., 1978.

————. *History of Eastern Christianity*. Rev. ed. 1980.

Bowman, A.K. *Egypt After the Pharaohs*. British Museum Publications, London, 1986.

Brooklyn Institute of Arts and Science Museum. *Late Egyptian and Coptic Art*. Brooklyn, New York, 1943.

Breasted, James. *A History of Egypt*. Hodder and Stoughton, London, 1950

Brown, Peter R.L. *The Making of Late Antiquity*. Harvard University Press, Cambridge, Mass., 1978.

————. *The Cult of the Saints, Its Rise and Function in Latin Christianity*. University of Chicago Press, 1981.

Butler, Alfred J. *The Ancient Coptic Churches of Egypt*. 2 vols. Clarendon Press, Oxford, 1884. New ed. 1970.

Carter, B.L. *The Copts in Egyptian Politics, 1918-1952*. The American University in Cairo Press, 1988.

Dodds, E.R. *Pagan and Christian in an Age of Anxiety*. W.W. Norton & Co., New York, London, 1970.

Evelyn-White, Hugh G. *The History of the Monasteries of the Wadi Natrun*. The Metropolitan Museum of Art, Egyptian Expedition. Cambridge University Press, 1933.

Gardiner, Sir Alan H. *Egypt of the Pharaohs*. Oxford University Press, 1961.

Gerspach, M. *Coptic Textile Designs*. Dover Publications, Inc., New York, 1975.

Hanna, Shenouda. *The Coptic Church, Symbolism and Iconography*. C. Tsoumas, Cairo, 1962.

Hardy, Edward R. *Christian Egypt*. Oxford University Press, 1952.

Jonas, Hans. *The Gnostic Religion: The Message of the Alien God and the Beginnings of Christianity*. Beacon Press, Boston, 2nd ed. 1963

Lane, Edward W. *The Manners and Customs of the Modern Egyptians*. East-West Publications, London, 1978.

Leeder, S.H. *Modern Sons of Pharaohs, A Study of the Manners and Customs of the Copts of Egypt*. Hodder & Stoughton, London, 1918.

Lewis, N. *Life in Egypt Under Roman Rule*. Oxford University Press, 1983.

Meinardus, Otto F.A. *Monks and Monasteries of the Egyptian Deserts*. The American University in Cairo Press, Rev. ed. 1989.

―――. *Christian Egypt, Ancient and Modern*. The American University in Cairo Press, 2nd ed. 1977.

―――. *Christian Egypt, Faith and Life*. The American University in Cairo Press, 1970.

Montet, P. *L'Egypte et la Bible*. Editions Delachaux & Niestlé, Neuchatel, 1959.

Oesterley, W.O.E. *The Wisdom of Egypt and the Old Testament.* Society for Promoting Christian Knowledge, London, 1927.

Pagels, E.H. *The Gnostic Gospels.* Random House, New York, 1979.

Peet, T.E. *Egypt and the Old Testament.* University Press of Liverpool, 1922.

Robinson, James M. Introduction in *The Nag Hammadi Library in English.* E.J. Brill, Leiden, 1977.

———. *The Coptic Gnostic Library: with English Translation, Introduction and Notes.* E.J. Brill, Leiden, 1975ff.

Sugden, E.H. *Israel's Debt to Egypt.* London, 1928.

Watkin, Edward. *A Lonely Minority. The Modern Story of Egypt's Copts.* Wm. Morrow & Co., New York, 1963.

Wilson, John A. *The Culture of Egypt.* University of Chicago Press, 1956.

Worrell, Wm.H. *A Short Account of the Copts.* University of Michigan Press, Ann Arbor, 1945.

INDEX

145